AF445379

The Pilots of Thunderbird Field

I walk hurriedly through the crowded Sky Harbor terminal, in Phoenix, Arizona, with my ten year old daughter, Lianne, by my side. We roll our luggage in tandem, each the competitive sort, trying to outpace the   other. Lianne's chuckle reverberations all through the terminal as we move along these lines and that method for evading approaching walkers.

go by Scott Weaver. I'm an American Airlines pilot and I am wearing full uniform today. Lianne admires me, appreciation filling her eyes. She's glad for me and the significant work I have yet adores how much fun I am, the means by which I am never reluctant to be senseless with her, particularly out traveling. She was brought into the world in China and was embraced by me and my better half when she was only a child.

As we race along, my cellphone rings. I stop to accept the call. "Put on your brakes, Lianne. You're not getting to the end goal before me!"

Lianne stops and keeping in mind that I talk into the telephone to American Airlines team planning about things that she cares very little about, she checks out the bustling terminal and notification a sparkly metal plaque holding tight a far divider. She is attracted to the plaque and strolls over to draw a nearer look. As she turns upward and checks the phrasing, her eyes augment in awe.

I surge over to her to reprimand her for strolling off. I advise her that she is to remain next to me. Things can happen quick, I was unable to bear to lose her, in addition to her mother would kill me. However, at ten, Lianne is godlike and gives no consideration to my talk. She is captivated in the plaque. She inquires as to whether this is the Thunderbird Field where her incredible granddad trained pilots to fly. I'm fairly shocked, astonished by her inquiry. I see she is gazing toward a plaque on the divider and I peer intently at it. The plaque recognizes Thunderbird Field, which was initially situated in Glendale close to the Sky

Harbor International Airport.

I react that Thunderbird Field was to be sure one of four landing strips around Phoenix. Lianne is flabbergasted when I tell her that the field was sold for one dollar. "It must be worth far beyond that, father. It was a significant spot where people were instructed to fly planes and battle a conflict, right?" And the shining metal plaque is evidence that Thunderbird Field was significant ! A short look of pity crosses her face. "You're correct, honey, it was a vital spot, however you'll discover that throughout everyday life, things can change and change quickly." I advise her that we discussed her incredible granddad when she was truly youthful. She cared barely at all about Thunderbird Field at that point yet presently that she's going with her dad, the pilot, and she is standing solidly in the very spot where her incredible granddad prepared pilots, Thunderbird promptly has another significance for her.

*Leo Purinton begins as a PT-17
flight teacher at Thunderbird Field
around 1942.*

Lianne recounts to me that she needs to hear the anecdote about her extraordinary granddad and the pilots of Thunderbird Field once more. I alert her that a story can't be told in a short time, which is her standard capacity to focus. Lianne demands she needs to hear everything. I consent to recount to her the anecdote about her extraordinary granddad, Leo Purinton, and the pilots of Thunderbird Field who he prepared yet remind her she should hear the whole story including about my granddad's more youthful days, how he turned into a pilot coach at Thunderbird Field and his job in World War II. Lianne is significantly more fascinated and invigorated and needs to hear the total story of her extraordinary granddad. I guarantee to let her beginning and end know when we get back.

I check the time. We need to hustle, our plane is booked to take off soon yet it will not take off except if I am there flying the American Airlines 737. Lianne beseeches me to allow her to sit in the cockpit however I advise her that it's contrary to the standards.

I bother her, "You are not a miscreant, are you?!" She snickers as I get a move on and surge down the terminal. Lianne rushes to advance beyond me and beat me to the door… and I let her.

Lianne and I are venturing out back to our home right outside of Washington DC after a concise working excursion. Lianne has been my companion on my 2-day succession DCA to DFW. DFW to PHX and back. She is situated in the five star area, close to the front of the plane. She lets the main airline steward know that she and her dad lived it up on their "excursion". They played in the pool, ate burgers and watched Toy Story, yet Lianne is certain that finding out with regards to Thunderbird Field will be the most awesome aspect of their excursion. She gladly lets the airline steward know that her incredible granddad was a "well known" man who prepared pilots at Thunderbird Field. At the point when the plane terrains, she is totally passed out. After different travelers have finished de-loading up and the airline stewards are wrapping up their last obligations, I stack Lianne's more modest bag on top of mine, get the dozing youngster, wrap her cautiously over my formally dressed shoulder and express profound gratitude to my team.

The following morning it is me who is zonked. A delicate pulling at my arm rouses me. I bust open one eye to be gazing straight in the delightful, dim sparkling eyes of my little girl. She advises me that I vowed to recount to her the anecdote about Thunderbird. I answer that it is six AM! I'm actually resting! She is tenacious lastly persuades her exceptionally sluggish dad out of his comfortable bed.

In the kitchen, I mishandle around for my dark espresso; it's an unquestionable requirement have for me in the first part of the day. Lianne holds on with arms crossed, tapping her foot eagerly hanging tight for her dad to finish his custom. I inquire as to whether she needs fried eggs or oat. She reacts that she doesn't need eggs or oat, she needs the story. What about blueberry hotcakes with chocolate sauce? Lianne's not having it. All she needs is the tale of her extraordinary granddad and the pilots of Thunderbird. Understanding that I am against headwinds that I can't move out of, I choose the family room love seat with some dark espresso and a young lady energetically anticipating to hear a story that is essential for her family's ancestry, part of the country's set of experiences.

Leo's first essential instructional course at Thunderbird I.

I let Lianne know that her extraordinary granddad was a World War II educator pilot. During the conflict, US, British and Chinese understudy pilots went to Thunderbird Field to gain proficiency with the strategies of flying in disaster areas and conveying their payloads. Leo Purinton was additionally resolute that these youthful cadets retain the significance of their central goal they were shielding their nations and safeguarding opportunity.

Those youthful understudy pilots were the most elite and had gone to Thunderbird to gain from the best. Lianne communicates her unexpected that Chinese pilots, similar to her kindred kinsmen, were pilots. I guarantee her that they were probably the sharpest and generally gifted and devoted pilots that her incredible granddad had prepared making Lianne blush and grin with satisfaction.

Chinese Cadets start essential preparing at Thunderbird I. Around 1942

I bring up how astounding the effect of Leo's preparation program at Thunderbird had been. Later ages of pilots from Leo's heredity proceeded to have assorted professions in flying. Lianne inquires as to whether my granddad prepared me. I clarify that I was a third era of pilots that had been enlivened by Leo's work. "Enlivened?" Lianne's not exactly certain what that implies. I help her to remember how she feels when she finishes one of her Lego palaces. Prodding her, I say "You know how you fantasy about turning into a designer when you grow up? That is being enlivened."

ianne snickers. She's very certain she never longed for turning into a designer, yet perhaps a modeler, yet assuming that she could possibly do, she's eternity adjusted her perspective. Presently she needs to be a pilot. I grin gladly - that is my young lady!

he offspring of Thunderbird - the in a real sense great many children and little girls who came after the first understudy pilots - proceeded to become military pilots in every one of the country's conflicts, business pilots for every one of the significant aircrafts of the world and to assume an essential part in putting the primary man on the moon. Lianne is captivated and needs to realize what her incredible granddad meant for the moon arrival. I advise her to show restraint; it's all essential for the family ancestry.

take a full breath and start the account of my granddad. How about we start when grandpa was brought into the world in 1910 in a modest community called La Junta, thirty or so miles east of Pueblo, Colorado, to a helpless family partying day in and day out in a nearby local area whose occupants generally shared the incline of monetary ruin. Everybody was metaphorically in almost the same situation. A railroad ran along the north

part of town consequently setting everybody on "some unacceptable" side of the tracks.

Leo Purinton and his family lived in a helpless modest little town in the Colorado dust bowl. Oklahoma wasn't the main state to make a case for that calamity in the works. The downturn that was reputed about didn't startle these people – as far as they could tell, they couldn't get any more unfortunate.

After Leo and his siblings, Glen and Jack, who were all nearby in age, overcame with their rudimentary training they longed for a day to day existence past La Junta. Their folks put stock in their children's capacities to make it all alone and set up no protection from their children's craving to look for a superior life. The young men were savvy, solid and ingenious; they would advance. Other than they had each other to rely on and it would be three less mouths to take care of for the striving family.

It was 1928, not long before the huge accident. While Wall Street hadn't done its notorious vanishing act yet, the normal individual in America was at that point feeling the sting of an imploding worldwide economy. Circumstances were difficult, cash was scant and food and fundamentals were an ordinary scrounger chase. Leo was a tall, solid young fellow and did all that he could to assist with keeping his family above water. He worked a few unspecialized temp jobs however at whatever point he and his siblings had free time they set out toward a stopgap storage around where they chipped away at their present object of fondness – an Eaglerock biplane fueled with a Glen Curtis planned OX-5 motor. An affluent farmer had bought the bi-plane yet lost interest in it – considering it a heap of garbage.

*Student pilot Leo Purinton
(sweater) before an
Eaglerock. 1927*

   Sensing that the Purinton young men were the perfect age and had a touch of the swashbuckler about them, the farmer permitted the young men to dabble with the plane with the expectation that they could get it up to speed and going. The young men thought it was Christmas morning when the farmer enlisted them to chip away at his plane and fly it, assuming they could get it air bound. To Leo and his siblings, the Eaglerock wasn't a heap of garbage – it was a fantasy and their expectation for what's to come.

Leo was a mechanical virtuoso and a characteristic for fixing things. His need was to get the plane going while Glen, the more seasoned of the two, ordinarily sat in the cockpit shouting out directions to Leo on the appropriate strategy for hand-wrenching a wooden propeller that would eventually be turning at risky and surprisingly close deadly degrees of speed. Glen left the ability part to Leo while he reclined in the cockpit and "administered" him. Glen wouldn't transparently let it out yet he realized that Leo had the smarts for fixing the plane and for understanding the mechanics of flying. Glen would trust that Leo will sort everything out so they might ultimately take off over the slopes and dales and look past the appearances of their little old neighborhood. Both young men were devoted enthusiasts of the Wright Brothers and tried to be important for the especially intriguing flight time. It was the world's future and it was their future.

Jack, Jimmy and Leo Purinton siblings
together before their Model Ford and
Travelair.
otice the turning prop

As young men Leo and his siblings partook in their lives in La Junta. In spite of the way that they cherished their folks and their different kin and would miss them, there came when the siblings detected that they had grown out of La Junta and the everyday and purposeless future it held for them. The time had come to proceed to strike out all alone. The siblings in the long run experienced their fantasy. Eighteen-year-old Leo and his more established siblings Glen and Jack bounced the train traveling west away, objective obscure. They had no particular plans and had just a single proviso about their future; it would include planes and flying!

The young men arrived in whatever humble communities and

networks that the trains they jumped on took them to. They kept on pushing toward the west and pursue

their fantasies about becoming pilots. As the years passed the young men had the option to find occupations at air terminals and sheds, learning however much they could at work and learning about aeronautics and planes all alone in whatever extra time they had. During the following ten years, their insight about flying developed as did their longing to be a genuine piece of the peculiarity. Getting by on a very tight budget income from their modest positions, they had the option to figure out sufficient cash to require incessant brief flying examples. They figured out how to steer little airplane developing their craving to cut out a vocation in flight. At last, two of the three siblings – Leo and Glen – proceeded to become regular citizen educator pilots at Thunderbird Field in Glendale, Arizona.

Brothers Jack and Leo before an Eaglerock

I give Lianne an intensive lesson on World War II and clarify how geo-political occasions prompted the establishing of the pilot preparing program at Thunderbird Field where her incredible granddad leaving an imprint for him and extraordinarily impacted what myself would one day seek after as a vocation. While Leo and his siblings remained fixed on their fantasy to turn out to be important for the consistently extending flying industry, the world was walking towards war.

n Europe, the threatening power snatch by the Nazis drove by Adolf Hitler was

turning into an expanding danger to the opportunity of US partners in Europe. At the point when the country of Belgium – a powerless country by military norms – was attacked and effortlessly taken over by the Nazis in 1940, Germany had adequately pronounced conflict on the remainder of Europe. Air power was an enormous variable in the struggles that followed. In excess of 50,000 Londoners were killed by bombs during German quick assault air strikes. In spite of the fact that US strategy drove by President Franklin Roosevelt appointed that the US was to stay nonpartisan, Great Britain and other European powers looked for the assistance of the US whose battling powers incorporated a high level air ability. At the point when the US was assaulted by Japan, a partner of Germany, at Pearl Harbor the country dropped its unbiased position and announced conflict on Germany and its partners and brought the entirety of its amazing military, both on the ground and noticeable all around, into the fight.

In 1942 during the lead-up to American association in the conflict, visionary US Army General Henry H. "Hap" Arnold quickly saw the requirement for people in the future of military pilots. He perceived that aeronautics would keep on growingly affecting the direct of battles later on and was vital for the security of the country. He tracked down the current preparing offices and capacities situated around the country as deficient in staying aware of that always expanding need. General Arnold visited the US to see direct exactly how insufficient the country's flight preparing program for military pilots was. It was surprisingly more terrible than he had envisioned.

Commanding General of the U.S. Armed force Air Forces, the main U.S. Aviation based armed forces general to hold five-star rank and whose thought it was for Thunderbird Field and other regular citizen preparing bases around the US.

With just a modest bunch of US Army Air Corps bases situated all through the country, there were just restricted preparing offices accessible for the foundation of a high level flying preparing program. General Arnold confronted a genuine situation. The managers of the country's handbag strings – the US Congress – had truth be told, exceptionally restricted financing put away for flying preparing. While congresspersons and agents could be censured for their absence of thinking ahead, it was the American individuals who might endure. The country would feel the effect of this lack of common sense except if the US pilot preparing program was upgraded and sped up.

It was hard to stand out enough to be noticed of the officials and the media for a

cause that General Arnold felt was critical for the security of the country. The General, consequently, chose to take the issue to general society. He zoomed around the nation communicating his interests and underlining the country's desperate requirement for pilot preparing offices and why it was fundamental that move be made right away. He refered to the bombings in London and different pieces of Europe that were killing individuals in large numbers. America must be ready to shield itself as powerfully via air as it safeguarded itself adrift and ashore.

Ultimately, General Arnold suggested that the central government go into contracts with private regular citizen preparing bases arranged around the country to foster the extraordinary number of skilled youthful pilots who were expected to assist the Allied Forces with shielding their opportunity in the European War. These instructional hubs were required to raise the avionics abilities and capacities of pilots who confronted the test of flying forays into the risky European and Pacific venues of World War II, the most crushing struggle at any point to confront man. General Arnold put forth a persuading defense and the public voiced its help for building up these private instructional hubs.

Chinese Cadets at Thunderbird Flightline

I look at Lianne at least a few times to ensure her eyes aren't coating over and that she is retaining my story. I guarantee her that disclosing the lead up to the conflict and the requirement for cutting edge air power was a basic piece of her

extraordinary granddad eventually turning into a teacher pilot. It was the conflict that moved the requirement for master pilots and it was that need that prompted the enlistment of top coaches with the information and mastery that would allow the pilots the best opportunity to become flying experts.

So it was the move by an Army General who perceived the need and the public who requested the foundation of preparing focuses that prompted the formation of pilot preparing focuses including Thunderbird Field. It was one of many instructional hubs that were set up across the southern states from Florida to California. With the US's entrance into the universal conflict, the developing public voice for activity constrained the US Congress to begin tossing genuine cash at preparing its tactical pilots.

*Leo's essential class at
Thunderbird I. Class "A"
regalia.*

The Pentagon and other government organizations started to bait financial specialists into putting resources into the preparation programs by promising to pay a generous measure of cash for each fruitful alumni. Eventually, more than 200,000 Americans were prepared as military pilots throughout only a couple of years. I reverberation Lianne's words at the air terminal when she demanded that Thunderbird was significant. Making these flying experts was indispensable in the triumph of the Allied

Forces over the Axis Powers. Without preparing focuses like Thunderbird Field and master coaches like Leo Purinton there might have been shocking outcomes
even loss – and the present world would be an altogether different spot. Lianne concurs, yet with however significant as it might have been, she thinks about how it might have been sold for a dollar. I react that numerous agreements are hard to comprehend.

*Under Chennault's order, The Chinese cadet started ground school at Thunderbird
Field*

Thunderbird Field

For the situation of Thunderbird Field, it had filled its need during the conflict and the lead ready. From that point forward, it had lost its motivation and in this way its worth. In April of 1946, Lieutenant General Barton Kyle Yount, the chief of the US Army Air Training Command, sanctioned Thunderbird Field to use for instructive purposes after the airbase was not generally required by the central government and proclaimed excess. Yount was the sole bidder on the property and thusly had the option to get Thunderbird Field for one dollar. The classes that were held at the new school which was named The American Institute for Foreign Trade started in October 1946. It was General Yount's fantasy to make the main US based worldwide business college that zeroed in on developing and teaching global business pioneers with establishes in both social traditions and sound business and the board rehearses. So is that the finish of the story, Lianne, inquires. I grin – by no stretch of the imagination! There's significantly more story to tell including the contribution of famous actors, my granddad's sentiment with an enchanting female pilot and the advancement of flying pros that would make the pilots in Top Gun could not hope to compare! Lianne is prepared and enthusiastic for additional! Lianne becomes flushed – my incredible granddad had a sentiment? I

react that obviously he did "How would you think I arrived?!"

he underlying thought for Thunderbird Field was the brainchild of three men, two of which one wouldn't consequently associate with the flight business. Thunderbird Field started in 1939 as a shared exertion between these three men from very surprising strolls throughout everyday life. However, the men made them thing in like manner – they were enthusiasts of the roaring aeronautics industry and right after a universal conflict approaching, they were devoted to guaranteeing the security of the country. These men were Hollywood specialist and maker Leland Hayward, previous Air Service pilot John H. "Jack" Connelly, and Life magazine picture taker John Swopes who together established Southwest Airways. The three preparing offices that involved Thunderbird Field were totally worked under the Southwest Airways umbrella.

PT-17 Thunderbird Ramp

The men went together to buy desert farmland found twenty miles from the boomtown of Phoenix, Arizona. The land was ruined and, from the get go, apparently shameful of any significant use. In any case, the men shared a fantasy and saw the desolate land was far beyond evaporated and deserted farmland. With just the deepest desires of an imaginative endeavor as far as they could tell, the men shaped an organization which they named Southwest Airways. It was a major dream and the chance of disappointment was more than the men were ready to voice. They were facing a challenge yet the danger was a commendable one – the country's very security was being referred to with the danger of war and loathsome designs to vanquish the world.

Southwest Airways
Owners, Jack Connelly
and Leland Hayward

The men pooled together a few thousand dollars that, even back then, was not an overwhelming sum for the establishing of another organization. In any case, what they needed financing they compensated for in steadiness and assurance. The men detected that they were leaving on a phenomenal excursion that could in a real sense shift the direction of history. With the impact of a Hollywood insider and the imaginative commitment of a picture taker, the men chose to make an instructional hub for military pilots that would be interesting and planned explicitly for the learners. The strangely organized complex contained holders and sleeping quarters that were spread out to take after the wings of a bird. The

control tower that was at the focal point of the complex was the head and eye of the bird. The long tail addressed the runway and landing region. Also, it was intended for the pilots in light of the fact that the picture of the thunderbird must be seen from the sky.

Thunderbird Mascot, Gigs

I had done some profound burrowing on Thunderbird Field and took in some new subtleties that gave a more extravagant, more unique image of the preparation office. The field was initially called

Thunderbird Field I and was worked by the Del Webb Construction Company in 1941. It was a working pilot preparing airbase through 1945, the year that denoted the finish of the conflict. Jay Thorne,

the ranking executive of interchanges for the Thunderbird School of Global Management had alluded to it as the runway that filled in as a "preparation site for worldwide World War II pilots."

Thunderbird Field is essential for America's celebrated flight history. It was considered an airbase that was "saturated with multicultural practice" with understudy pilots from America, Canada, Britain and China. Nearby Field I, there were different landing strips in the valley that were likewise utilized for preparing. Those fields included Thunderbird Field II which at last became Scottsdale Airport and Falcon Field in Mesa, Arizona. The field at Mesa was initially called Thunderbird Field III yet since the office would be committed to the preparation of British pilots, the Brits inquired as to whether they could name it after one of their native birds. Along these lines, Thunderbird III became Falcon Field. More than a $1 million of every 1940 dollars was initially raised to assemble the base.

Local Native American Chief Wipala
Wicki and the Thunderbird logo.
Around 1942

Scottsdale Airport was initially established on June 22, 1942 as Thunderbird Field II. It was the essential preparing office for World War II Army Air Corps pilots. The grounds were changed from a little land parcel in the far off Arizona desert into a state of the art preparing office that made some meaningful difference ever. Two visionary pioneers – General H.H. Arnold and Lieutenant General B. K. Yount – are credited with this change. The commitments of Leyland Hayward and John Connelly who worked the regular citizen contract school were additionally instrumental in the preparation office's achievement. Together these men were devoted to giving the best preparing and eventually assisted with building the most impressive airborne striking power that the world had at any point seen. In spite of the fact that Thunderbird Field preparing offices were producing flying pros dangerously fast, there was consistently strain to accomplish more. As the conflict mists thickened over Europe, the quantity of cadet pilots to be prepared expanded with each new class that was planned. In November 1943, the instructional hub was working at top limit, preparing 615 cadets who timed a normal of two flight hours daily which converted into 1,845 separate departures and a long time of thorough in-class preparing.

Despite the strain to deliver an ever increasing number of qualified pilots, Thunderbird Field just filled in its standing for serious and careful guidance and for creating the top flying pros on the planet. At last, Thunderbird II graduated more than 5,500 understudies which beat unique assumptions by the Air Force triple. All in all Thunderbird II pilots flew almost 26,500,000 miles which is what might be compared to surrounding the earth multiple times! Those details addressed the magnificence long periods of Thunderbird Field II yet the instructional hub's time was restricted. Subsequent to working for a very long time, 90 days and 24 days, Thunderbird Field II was closed down.

There was an optional reason for the unique plan of Thunderbird Field and that was the making of a strange and eye-engaging set for a future Hollywood film. With a Hollywood specialist being important for the principal architects of Southwest Airways, thinking back it was practically inescapable that a touch of marvelousness and dramatization would be essential for the blend. The film, which was likewise created in 1942, that very year that Southwest Airways was established, was called Thunder Birds – which destined the plan design of the complex. It was regular that the real runway was named for the enormous "bird" that could be seen distinctly from a higher perspective. Thunderbird Field arose among the many new preparing fields as exceptional and by a wide margin the most renowned. It was the spot to be. It was figuratively the "bubbling energy source everyone crowds around" contrasted with the other more sullen and less captivating instructional hubs. Jimmy Stewart, who had enlisted in the US Air Force during the conflict exertion, was instrumental in the foundation of the field and in pointing out it. Big names came to Thunderbird Field and celebrated until the extremely early times.

Actor Jimmy Stewart getting Air Medal

There were swing groups and sumptuous social occasions of the popular. Old Hollywood made Thunderbird Field their selective desert escape. Maybe the celebrating and festivity belieed the pressure that was noticeable all around and the expectation of war that lingered over the country. Furthermore, however there were a lot of beverages and chuckles and fun occasions at these gatherings, everybody was significantly mindful that Thunderbird Field had a considerably more significant job in the fate of America. The field would figure as one of the quiet saints of the conflict exertion. The pro pilots that Thunderbird Field turned out were a critical component in the Allied triumph over Axis powers and Nazism. In any case, as the Hollywood stars moved and celebrated, nobody had any assurance regarding what world they would be confronted with after the conflict, particularly in the alarming possibility of rout. America was glad and secure with itself yet it had until recently never been assailed with the malicious test drove by Adolf Hitler. While Hollywood made conflict motion pictures in which the Axis powers were crushed, the remainder of America was encountering a transitionary period. The country was at long last in the last phases of recuperation from the monetary and social catastrophe brought forth by the Great Depression. With scarcely a flicker of the eye, this post-misery time was supplanted by a country that was very nearly universal conflict. The military was fortifying its numbers and making arrangements for what the Pentagon knew would be the greatest wartime challenge that the country had at any point confronted.

On one hand times were great – joblessness was low, breadlines had vanished and the common individual was appreciating life without precedent for many years. In any case, then again, war was approaching and assuming the US went into the conflict that was seething in Europe, life for some, families could never go back again.

Although Thunderbird Field addressed the battle against global control by the Nazis, it was likewise a splendid recognize, an encouraging sign for the country and people in the future. The office was set up to end up master pilots who might forfeit their very lives to protect their kinsmen. Following quite a while of tough situations there was an option that could be greater than the person that everybody could be a piece of. Not at all like conflicts that followed World War II, similar to Vietnam, the country met up on the side of the conflict exertion and its daring warriors including the first class pilots who were to assume a gigantic part in the Allied triumph. Maybe it was not voiced however the vast majority realized that the actual eventual fate of the world depended in huge part on the effective missions of the men and

ladies who might go through the entryways of Thunderbird Field. Essential Pilot Training instructed at Thunderbird covered flight rudiments utilizing two-seater preparing airplane. This underlying phase of preparing was by and large educated by teachers from contract non military personnel pilot preparing schools through the Civil Aeronautics Authority, War Training Service (CAA-WTS). Cadets normally were needed to procure 60 to 65 flight hours in Stearman, Ryan or Fairchild essential coaches prior to happening to Basic Training. Fundamental Pilot Training shrouded guidance in flying in line, by instruments or by airborne route, around evening time and for significant distances. Cadets by and large timed around 70 flight hours in BT-9 or BT-13 essential coaches before they were endorsed to happen to Advanced Training.

dvanced Training was isolated into two significant classes: single-motor and multi-motor. Those cadets in the single-motor program fled 6 progressed coach. The cadets in the multi-motor gathering figured out how to fly the AT-9, AT-10, AT-11 or AT-17 progressed coaches. Cadets in cutting edge preparing were relied upon to hoard 75 to 80 flight hours prior to being qualified for graduation when they would accept their pilot's wings. Change Pilot Training progressed single-motor pilots to warriors and contender planes and multi-motor pilots to transports or aircraft. The aggregate sum of preparing time before pilot cadets were sent into dynamic battle obligation was two months.

Chinese Cadets 43-K

Training at Thunderbird was requesting and the understudy pilots who prepared there were committed and very much aware of their part in the conflict and in protecting their nation yet were young fellows who jumped at the chance to have some good times. They frequently indulged themselves with some recreation time on the ends of the week from their instructional hub that was in a real sense in no place and gave little freedom to having a great time. A significant number of the youthful fliers would jam into vehicles and travel the twenty miles to Phoenix where they could let free a bit and leave the pressure of requesting preparing behind them. They could partake in a warm dinner and a cool brew without stresses of getting up the following day at first light to confront a drawn out day of thorough preparing and study hall work where they would find out with regards to the missions that they were being prepared for.

The genuine delight for pilots who had finished the preparation program was the festival that followed the graduation service. Cadets were urged to welcome their families, spouses and lady friends to the merriments. In the Ballroom the youngsters would move to Big Band music. Regularly Hollywood stars were welcome to go to graduation festivities. They would fly out to be essential for the scene much to the rush and enjoyment of the cadets and their visitors. From Hollywood lights to the customary person in the city there was inescapable help for the conflict. Hollywood stars like Clark Gable and numerous others upheld the soldiers by visiting the nation and selling US depository bonds. It was a public development. As opposed to the sharpness that America held for later conflicts, it was surprising looking back that there was such inescapable help of the country's interest in the conflict. The individuals who upheld the conflict considered it to be indispensable for the propagation of life as far as they might be concerned.

An instructional hub pamphlet just named, "The Thunderbird" was given consistently. Qualities like serving and positive energy were normal topics found in articles remembered for these pamphlets. In one article in the December 1943 issue, the cozy connection among pilot and plane technician was engaged upon. That equivalent issue promotes the devoted tenor of Southwest Airways' workers who put adding to the conflict exertion more significant than what they were paid.

Chinese graduation.
Class 43-C

Letters from previous Thunderbird cadets who were on the conflict front were likewise referred to in the bulletins to fill in as guides to the cadets in preparing that they would see activity on the conflict front. The bulletins were expected to keep up the assurance of the cadets going through requesting preparing and to in-still in them the soul of nationalism. While the in-class preparing and flight hours showed them how to fly, these bulletins worked at instilling positive qualities in the pilots accordingly putting the final details on the pro pilots emerging from preparing and going to the risks of the genuine front line. In every bulletin Thunderbird's roll of honor talked about military pilots who had moved on from Thunderbird and the significant jobs they were playing in the War being battled with regards to majority rules system. One pamphlet detailed that as per official military public statements there was a stamped expansion in the quantity of Thunderbird graduates in deployment ready on the conflict front. Alumni of the preparation office were serving on five mainlands and on task in such different areas as Alaska, Guadalcanal, Africa and England. The article gladly recorded the references and adornments that Thunderbird graduated class were acquiring. Such articles motivated the cadets at present in preparing who read these articles. The youthful pilots were dauntless and enthusiastic and anxious to traverse preparing and onto the war zone.

Chinese cadets graduation day

Knowing that Lianne would be keen on the Chinese cadet pilots who had moved on from Thunderbird Field, I read to her an article in an old Thunderbird bulletin about the seventh class of Chinese cadets who had finished their essential preparing. Albeit the cutting edge connection between the US and China is a shaky one, best case scenario, during World War II there was a certifiable collegial collaboration between the two nations, a lot of which was because of the numerous Chinese aviators who were prepared through the Thunderbird preparing offices.

In an emblematic signal to show the kindness between the nations during the lead up to World War II and real commitment in the contention, China's dearest First Lady, Madame Chiang Kai-shek, honored Thunderbird for giving the essential preparing of all the country's flying corps cadets. She would have liked to visit the offices herself however because of medical affliction she had to offer her recognition from Los Angeles.

Madame Chiang Kai-shek, lovingly known as Missimo by the Chinese public, remembered for her accolade for the instructional hub the introduction of the Chinese banner that would fly with the American banner to represent the two country's fortitude. China was at incredible danger in the Pacific Theater because of the danger of a forceful and aggressive Japan which had aligned with Germany. It was fundamental that China's flying corps be reinforced and extended which constrained the country to go to America and Thunderbird for the best preparing that was accessible.

Peter Stackpole, youthful Chinese cadet, picture taken by Life magazine

Lianne is propelled by the tale of the Chinese pilots prepared at Thunderbird Field. Despite the fact that she adores her folks, she has a developing interest in her Chinese heritage and is anxious to find out about Chinese history and culture. I perceive the incongruity that whenever she first makes a genuine association with that culture is through flight - something that connects her with both her family and her Chinese legacy.

I tell Lianne that I took in a ton about Thunderbird Field and about my granddad by perusing Leo's flight log books. I felt like I was encroaching into an extremely close to home time in my granddad's life, occasions that held a lot of importance in his life. It was a period that turned into a piece of the country's set of experiences. Leo kept a journal that was generally centered around the triumphs and quantities of fights flown every day. Leo had fostered a shorthand that permitted him with simply a word or two to depict the day's exercises. Leo was careful with regards to staying up with the latest.

Collection of Leo's flying log books and that's just the beginning.

Perhaps an idea or two might have streaked through his brain that some time or another person may coincidentally find his journal convincing him to ensure that it was comprehensive. During the time-frame that would have been the lead up to the conflict, Leo logged upwards of six or seven, one-hour or longer trips for every day. He would list the names of the pilot understudies who flew every one of the preparation missions. I stumbled into words like ground circle, pinked, turns, slows down, washed back and surprisingly the names of Hollywood entertainers to which extraordinary importance probably been appended, implying that has been lost in the mediating years. Leo additionally noticed the occasions that happened every day and guests who halted by – regularly it was a big's name that was written down under "guests."

I grin at Lianne and say, "Presently for the sentiment."

Lianne snickers and is listening eagerly. At the point when I was going over my granddad's logbooks, I detected a name that showed up frequently – "Spot." I normally became inquisitive with regards to who for sure Dot was and why the word was so

conspicuous in Leo's log books. Was it a thing or an individual – possibly 1940s' shoptalk? In the wake of delving into more logs and finding some close to home letters, I at long last sorted out that the reference to "Spot" was short for Dorothea, Dorothea Rexroad who was Leo's subsequent spouse.

Leo with his subsequent spouse,
Doretha, "Dab" and
his cadets

Dot grabbed the attention of the youthful educator for her magnificence, insight and for the love of flight that they shared. Leo was defenseless at that point. He was harming from the deficiency of his young spouse who had passed on in labor. The couple had an eight-year-old girl, Alyce, when Leo's significant other kicked the bucket attempting to bring forth Alyce's younger sibling. Unfortunately, mother and child both kicked the bucket and Leo was sadness blasted and distressed and confronted an existence without an accomplice. He had to assume the difficult obligation of bringing up a youthful girl while withstanding the pressure of his requesting position.

Lacking an emotionally supportive network, Leo regularly carried little Alyce to Thunderbird Field with him. She would play with her dolls and shading books at the rear of the room while he showed the understudies.

Alyce presumably accidentally acquired information about avionics simply being in the homeroom and presented to her dad's talks again and again. Lianne calls attention to that I just took her to work actually like her extraordinary granddad did with his little girl. The correlation makes me grin. Appears there was something else to his granddad's ancestry besides aviation.After I found that the many "Speck" documentations alluded to Leo's subsequent spouse, I chose to ask my mom, Alyce, about her. Alyce recollected Dot as a

dazzling lady who Leo had met and immediately succumbed to. She before long turned into a consistent presence in the Purinton family. Leo, still in grieving over the spouse he cherished and lost and lamenting over the passing of a kid, invited Dot into his life. She mended his injured heart with her appeal and friendship and he before long saw her as his possible spouse.

Knowing that Leo's pride was in his avionics abilities, I imagined my granddad dazzling Dot with a twist in his private Travelair, presumably picking the circumstance of the radiant Arizona dusk to give most extreme dramatization to the ride. Possessing a private plane was an extraordinariness back then. Speck must be excited having an attractive youthful admirer who not exclusively was a pilot yet who possessed his own airplane. Any little youngster's head would turn. Behind the façade of Leo's own appeal and breathtaking profession, was a youngster who was all the while going through the last phases of misery and who was confronting a pile of liability. He had an eight-year-old young lady to raise without help from anyone else and was committed to a vocation that he cherished. Leo took on the extra pressure fashioned by the developing significance of his work as the nation walked on to war. He wanted an accomplice to help him. Leo came from fair stock and never utilized anybody. He went gaga for Dot however he additionally required an accomplice. The presence of the hidden double purposes that prompted their marriage didn't detract from the genuine love he had in his heart for Dot.

As I dove further in my exploration about Dot and her relationship with Leo, I discovered that Dot eventually turned into a Woman Air Force Service Pilot or WASP in the US Army and graduated with her flying endorsement from Texas State University. Hence while Leo might have had his reasons past his authentic love for Dot, she additionally had her own reasons past passionate ones for being attracted to him. While he was romancing Dot, he was additionally encouraging her to fly. While their common love for avionics might have at first united them, in the end it was basically to a limited extent answerable for their separation. After Dot figured out how to fly she felt a call to accomplish more.

Dorothea Rexroad with Chinese cadet.
Circa 1944

There were additionally pressures in the Purinton family since Dot didn't attempt to support a relationship with little Alyce. The marriage endured under a year. Speck followed her fantasy to serve her nation and became one of the main female pilots entrusted with the significant occupation of moving B-26s from US industrial facility floors to the conflict front in Europe. It was a concise relationship yet for Leo it got him through some difficult stretches. He cherished Dot yet he comprehended that in light of that affection he needed to release her. Dab had no second thoughts – she figured out how to fly amidst an astonishing sentiment. Spot imparted a fate to numerous other young ladies of her time. Things were changing in the country's social mores; it was a period for ladies to play a bigger job in guarding the country. However numerous ladies did significant positions in the processing plants making ammo and collecting planes, others made a stride past that. Spot was one of those ladies. The WASP, filled in as a feature of the Army Air Force all through US contribution in World War II -

from September 1942 through December 1944 when the Allied Forces were triumphant over the Axis Powers. In excess of 1,000 ladies had served their country in this limit. Lianne inquires as to whether the Air Force actually had a unit for ladies. I react that society had

progressed a considerable amount from that point forward. Presently young ladies can enlist in the Air Force and not be put in an exceptional unit for ladies. Lianne is dazzled – she'll recall that for future reference!

W.A.S.P. logo planned by Walt Disney

My dad and Lianne's granddad, Richard "Doc" Weaver remained consistent with family custom and cut out a long vocation in avionics for himself. Richard was in ROTC at San Jose State in the mid 1950s when he met Leo's little girl, Alyce Purinton. Obviously she would later turn into my mom and Lianne's grandma. Richard had a similar liking for flying and flying as Alyce's dad did. Prior to going to undergrad pilot preparing (UPT) at Laredo AFB in Texas he finished his private pilot's endorsement in Eurika, Oregon, where Leo was a teacher. It had been a long time since Leo had shown cadet pilots at Thunderbird Field. That time was finished and however Leo left behind numerous recollections in the ten years he was there, he was glad for his achievements and perceived that the time had come to continue on.

One thing that Leo could never leave behind was his adoration for flight. Any profession that he chose to seek after consistently elaborate flight. Leo was a specialist pilot and a committed and patient educator. It was normal, accordingly, for him to proceed with his contribution with aeronautics and continue on to Oregon where he had the chance to set up his originally Fixed Based Operation (FBO) in the

state. One of Leo's first understudies was the youthful Richard Weaver. The exceptional preparing that Richard got from Leo set him on a profession way in the US Air Force during which he had the chance to fly a wide assortment of airplane including the KC97, the KC135, the C123 and the T39.

Richard Weaver saw battle obligation during the years 1965 and 1966. He fled, a little twin-motor travel during the Vietnam struggle. He moved everything from troops,weapons and mail for the soldiers to the lethal Agent Orange, a defoliant that was utilized on the Ho Chi Minh trail, the course the North Vietnamese used to move ammo and supplies to the war zone in the south. By dispersing the thick development that encompassed the Ho Chi Minh, the US military had the option to uncover Viet Cong and North Vietnamese guerrillas whose strategy was to take out US and South Vietnamese troopers expert sharpshooter style from the front of the thick underbrush. By lessening the viability of the North's close quarters combat on the path, the exchange of provisions from the Vietcong was significantly diminished. Richard's commitment to the conflict exertion was an illustration of the flexibility and significance of air influence in one more conflict.

After his responsibilities regarding the Vietnam War exertion finished, Richard was allocated on a deployment supporting NASA somewhere in the range of 1967 and 1970 in which he flew an adjusted Boeing 707. The mission of this visit was to screen space travelers during the Apollo program utilizing a particular interchanges framework which his 707 was furnished with.

Lianne didn't know about exactly the number of other relatives at last turned out to be important for the flying business. To repeat to a limited extent, there was the patriarch of the family pilots – Leo who was a pilot educator at Thunderbird Field in Arizona. Leo's subsequent spouse, Dot Rexroad, eventually turned into a pilot, a WASP and B26 pilot during the conflict. Leo's child and my dad, Lt. Colonel Richard Weaver was a pilot, Vietnam veteran and a help pilot for NASA. Leo's more seasoned sibling, Jimmy Purinton was likewise a Thunderbird teacher, traveler, Hollywood trick pilot just as one of the primary business pilots in Oregon.

The 13 Black Cats were adrenaline junkie flyers who worked for Howard Hughes who had his own relationship with flight. These flyers were the first Barnstormers after World War I who flew planes into trees, structures, changed "punctured tires" midair, played tennis on top of wings and wing strolled also. Flying from one homestead to another, stable to animal dwellingplace, was the means by which the country's first flying thrill seekers got their name. Leo and his sibling Jimmy did some trouping

and may have encountered the popular company. My incredible uncle flew at Thunderbird Field as an educator and was an additional an in Hughes' 1930 film Hell's Angels, an anecdote about RAF pilots who protected the British Crown during World War I. It was here, flying as "additional items" in the film business, where the Purinton siblings presumably encountered the country's first popular Barnstormers, the 13 Black Cats. The fabulousness of Hollywood and the energy and risk of flying was a characteristic blend and started in the beginning of the avionics age. This combination of Hollywood wizardry and the appeal of aeronautics has been kept up with consistently. The exemplification of this enamoring combination was found in the famous film about flying pros, Top Gun, a film which inspired me to join the USAF in the mid 1980's.

Lianne is a splendid young lady and normally perceives the extraordinary chance that she also would continue in the family's custom and seek the skies for a vocation. Following a lot of time narrating, Lianne is worn out and languid yet amped up for her family's story. She nods off before her head hits the cushion that evening. I grin, kiss her on the temple and pull the concealment over her. "Sweet dreams, dear."

The following morning I feel like it's this feels familiar!! One eye opens up when I feel a pulling on my arm. It's Lianne again all splendid and gleaming following a decent night's rest. I whine that I told her beginning and end I have some familiarity with about my granddad, Thunderbird Field and our family's long contribution in avionics. In any case, Lianne isn't requesting that I recount her more stories-she has a story to tell me.

I sit up and pull Lianne up in bed. Energetically she lets me know that she is sure that she will likewise one day be a pilot. She had a fantasy... she was a young lady in China, strolling through a bustling carrier terminal and wearing a pilot's uniform!

She had quite recently handled a cutting edge business aircraft into Beijing and it was the year 2042! I pay attention. For what reason did she say it was 2042?! The year 2042 would be the 100th commemoration of the establishing of Thunderbird Field yet I'd never referenced that to Lianne. I ask Lianne how she realized that it was 2042. She lets me know it was the plaque on the divider – very much like the plaque they found in the air terminal in Arizona.

Lianne's face becomes genuine. She lets me know that in her fantasy she detected the plaque from across the terminal and similarly as she had done in Arizona when she was a young lady she was attracted to it. She read the plaque that recognized the commitments of the Chinese Pilots in WWII and their US Instructor Pilots. Lianne recalls the day she strolled through the Sky Harbor

Airport in Phoenix. In her fantasy state, she felt somewhat tragic for a couple of seconds however at that point grinned. She was unable to see them – the pilots in her family, however she realized they were for the most part present for her – for the most part present in soul, cherishing and supporting her and pleased that she was proceeding in the family custom. Lianne woke up with a major grin, acknowledging what a magnificent dream it was.

RAF's Yellow Pearl

O ne afternoon I returned from Buenos Aires and, though I enjoyed

the trip, as always I was happy to be home again. I was exhausted as I pulled into the driveway and headed for the front door, stopping to pick up the mail.

Once inside, I threw the mail down on the control center table in the hall aiming to pass on it for my significant other to open. I left however at that point halted. My eye had discovered something surprising. I turned around and detected a lovely looking envelope addressed to the family and written in an exquisite adapted content. I painstakingly opened the envelope and saw that it was a wedding greeting. At 54, Jez, a close buddy and individual pilot would at last be wedding his long-term love, Sarah. The wedding would be occurring in London.

I knew promptly that my significant other wouldn't have the option to make the excursion. She is a lawyer who works at the National Institutes of Health as a counsel to the nation's top specialists and researchers. She had a bustling forthcoming timetable and would not have any spare energy to make the excursion.

But it would be the ideal excursion for myself as well as my more seasoned little girl, Sybille (Syb) who is 25, to take together. I'd pilot our flight and Syb would be directly behind me in the "cowhide" or top of the line or business class. I realized she'd be anxious to go. Syb is stepping in family custom and has desires to turn into an airline steward and is consistently anxious to go with me on any of my global flights. Also, she'd appreciate being in London once more. She has a broad global foundation – indeed, Europe was her first home. Sybille Marie Weaver was brought into the world in Chartres, France on 2 April 1991.

fter moving to the states, Syb went to the Lycée Rochambeau, a

esteemed private French School in Bethesda, MD. Later she and her mom and stepdad moved to Sao Paulo, Brazil where Syb moved on from Graded High School. She communicates in English, French and Portuguese and went to college in Montreal for one year. She presently lives in the Raleigh, NC region and is right now working at being acknowledged into a nursing program – however the fantasy about being essential for the flying business actually waits.

As a little youngster, she would go this way and that from DC to Paris with

her sibling consistently on AA representative passes. She is an extremely wonderful and worldwide young woman with binds to France, US and Brazil. At the point when we got the greeting, Syb was living in North Carolina. I realized she was on a break from work and that she'd have adequate downtime to have the option to make the outing with me. I gave her a speedy call and informed her concerning the greeting. As I anticipated, she was amped up for proceeding to anticipate the outing.

Jez Hopkinson with Team Yaks 50 and 52

Jez is a pilot prepared by the RAF. He is a genuine person with a cordial character. He can be an enchanting person yet now and again can be somewhat of a serious annoyance and I am not hesitant to say as much! Be that as it may, regardless of his imperfections, Jez is a dear companion, similar to a sibling, and similarly as essential to me, an incredible flyer and admirer of flight – simply my sort of fellow. Jez was an educator with the RAF during the 1980s yet presently has his own group of demo flyers, called Team Yakovlevs. The group flies Russian constructed Yak-50s and Yak 52s and they show up at presentations

all throughout the planet including England, Europe, India and China. Thinking back on the historical backdrop of Thunderbird, I can't resist the urge to think how little this enormous wide world truly is. Jez and his RAF prepared demo group have visited all throughout the planet yet the RAF had its beginnings at Thunderbird Field.

It was going great on the long outing to England without any "knocks" in the gauge. It offered me the chance to partake in the outing and have some an ideal opportunity to connect with Syb. I value minutes like this when I can require some investment to think and let it hit home exactly that I am so fortunate to have a vocation that permits me to see the world and a family that upholds me living life to the fullest. I particularly relish events like this when I'm at the harsh with an individual from my family unit on board. It makes my work even more pleasant and fulfilling that I'm ready to give a protected trip to my friends and family. Not that I don't generally partake in my work. I love it – like ages in my family before me – needed nothing other than a vocation in flight. In any case, the obligation of a plane loaded up with many travelers normally tends to welcome on a little tension – Syb being on board on this flight removed a portion of the air from that strain. As different travelers welcomed me with, "Hey, Captain," or "extraordinary flight" or even a wisecracker to a great extent advising me to get back at the controls, I grinned at my little girl who comprehended the significant connection among pilot and traveler. It had for quite some time been my fantasy that she'd have a vocation in flight. It has been Syb's fantasy, as well; presently it has turned into her aspiration and genuine objective.

The routine outing likewise gave personal opportunity to ponder Jez and the celebrated custom of the RAF pamphlets, a large number of whom went through the unbelievable Thunderbird and Falcon Fields in the US. This outing was allowing me the opportunity to partake in the present, ponder the future and think about the past.

My considerations promptly went to an old RAF flyer who I knew would be in participation at the wedding – Sarah's distant uncle who everybody – loved ones the same – tenderly called Uncle Sam. The wedding would be occurring on an old homestead in Ashford that had been in Sarah's family for ages. Uncle Sam was remaining on the ranch in a little cabin – sort of administering things however giving him reason in his last years and furnishing him with a delightful spot to live. I had been at the ranch and in and around Ashford a few times before. It is noteworthy, as numerous things in Great Britain are. Ashford is southeast of London en route to Dover where the Battle of Britain occurred in 1940 during World War II.

I'd got together with Uncle Sam a couple of times during my visits. He is the thing that everybody considers as the commonplace Brit –

glad, refined and a little

haughty, disapproving of a piece at Americans. Despite the fact that I'm an American, he was consistently glad to see me. I address another person, somebody who he can recount his accounts to on the grounds that his loved ones had heard them all over and again! Furthermore, I am somebody who partook in his accounts, even the retreads, and am consistently glad to tune in. Nothing gives me more joy than to catch wind of the encounters of a RAF pilot who'd served in World War II.

Battle of Britain, Air protection safeguard, 1940

Although Uncle Sam is almost ninety, his eyes actually light up at seeing a beautiful young lady; they presumably help him to remember his greatness years as a RAF pilot and one of the UK's public saints. At the point when my beautiful little girl showed up at the ranch for the wedding, that shine in his eye returned. We originally experienced Uncle

Sam at a supper the night prior to the wedding. He had a lot of stories to tell. In spite of the fact that I'd heard all of Uncle Sam's conflict stories on a few events previously and numerous comparable stories from other veteran pilots, I was hearing them again when I brought my girl for the wedding. It never pestered me that he was telling stories I'd effectively heard; I felt respected and had the feeling that I was coming to back and strolling with history, or for this situation, flying with it. I appreciated hearing the tales again and seeing the old noble man reconnect with a great past.

Uncle Sam sat among me and Syb at the supper. He thought back with regards to his time at Falcon Field, grinning at the amusing tales he imparted to us and reviewing the tough preparing program that certified him as a RAF pilot. He adored vehicles nearly however much he cherished planes. He welcomed us to stop by his place the following daytime promising to show us what he alluded to as the Yellow Pearl, a vintage Cadillac from the days prior to the conflict that he actually claimed. Syb was captivated by his memories of being an additional an in bygone era war films and fraternizing with big names of the day. I especially delighted in finding out about his cooperations with my granddad, Leo Purinton and distant uncle Jimmy Purinton, who were the two teachers when Uncle Sam prepared at the amazing Falcon Field.

As the night wore on and the champagne streamed, Uncle Sam became solemn. Not all accounts from his avionics vocation evoked warm recollections. Tears overflowed in his eyes when he talked about the desolation of losing his RAF flat mate in a preparation mishap. He enlightened us regarding meeting his first love during preparing. The relationship didn't withstand time and distance and the bad dream of war. Notwithstanding the couple of tears that streaked down his cheeks, in general Uncle Sam partook in the evening and the numerous great recollections that characterized his life and profession.

The following morning we strolled over to his little lodge. Uncle Sam showed us up into the space where the dividers were covered with memorabilia from his spell as a RAF pilot. He opened an old trunk which was in a real sense gushing out over with photographs, log books, news stories, outfits, awards and letters.

"Uncle Sam," I prodded him, "I'll bet there's a couple of affection letters in that reserve."

Uncle Sam took a gander at me seriously, an obvious gleam in his expression, "In excess of a couple, youngster," he reacted. "In excess of a couple."

Syb and I snickered. Unexpectedly, old Uncle Sam looked intently at a pile of photographs and got one of them.

"Look here!" Uncle Sam said with a major smile. "From my days at Falcon Field. The young lady in this photograph looks actually like you, Syb."

We all took a gander at the photograph. There was simply the smallest similarity to Syb yet Uncle Sam was having a happy time reviewing recollections from another time I would have rather not ruin his fun so I concurred that the young lady looked a ton like Syb.

"Two delights certainly" Uncle Sam said.

With a recharged energy from the response from his drew in and young guests, Uncle Sam started to look cautiously through his memorabilia. He gladly showed us his RAF wings. The Royal Air Force's wings are fabric not normal for the US wings which are made of metal. At the point when the cadets moved on from pilot preparing at Falcon Field the primary thing they did was have their wings sewn on their uniform. The US Army and USAF allude to it as the "nailing to function." The British are significantly more conventional – some would call it stodgy. RAF pilots invest wholeheartedly in their additional tedious "sewing-on service" to appropriately show their well deserved pilot wings on their garbs. Generally, the new RAF pilot had his better half, sweetheart or mother do the distinctions of sewing on the wings. In any case, Falcon Field

was a significant stretch from England and, obviously, a universal conflict was seething. The greater part of the RAF cadets couldn't stand to have their spouses or other relatives go to their graduations furthermore it wasn't protected to go around then.

I knew promptly that Syb saw the RAF wings only as old grimy and blurred badge yet to Uncle Sam they addressed what was to him the high mark of his life. I totally comprehended his sentiments. Numerous people in my family had associations with aeronautics and the valorous pilots of World War II. It was the last conflict that the public upheld and the last officers who general society invited back as legends who had safeguarded their countries from the mistreatment and evil of Nazi animosity. Syb couldn't start to comprehend the profundity of feelings that was at the center of the recollections that had become so settled in Uncle Sam's cognizance. Furthermore, I wouldn't anticipate that she should. I was more ready to completely see the value in Uncle Sam's accounts and sentiments about his experience since I was a pilot and in light of the fact that so many among loved ones preceding me were pilots, a significant number of whom were pilots in the World War. Uncle Sam's association with Falcon Field was a solid string that associated both of us and it was a connection that would never be broken. There was an esprit des corps that grew naturally from our preparation, experience and administration.

RAF cadets has Arizona
sweetheart "nail to" his
wings

Through his memories, Uncle Sam was changed once again into the bold pilot he used to be. As he recounted his story, he nearly appeared to seem more youthful. He discussed subtleties that my little girl could easily forget and that I alone could completely appreciate. Uncle Sam recounted the story how consistently as a RAF cadet he would have Friday night and Saturday off – a brief however essential rest from the requesting pilot preparing program.

Falcon Instructors and staff. Plateau, Az.

Uncle Sam affectionately reviewed the warm gathering he and the other RAF cadets got from the groups of the Mesa people group. History makes many references to the Allied Forces of World War II, yet there were solid connections far that went a long ways past the military. It was likewise the residents of those countries battling against the Axis Powers who were similarly as unified in their help of the reason. The warm and ardent gathering that the RAF pilots delighted in from individuals of Mesa was nevertheless one little illustration of the association that individuals on the Allies felt from one side of the planet to the other during the conflict.

local people would line the street outside Falcon Field as the cadets left the front door in order to support a cadet for the end of the week. Those cadets who were supported partaken in an end of the week around with their new Arizona loved ones. It caused them to feel appreciated and clearly it gained lovely experiences that endured forever. Numerous connections that started during RAF preparing in

Falcon Field did endure forever. In those days individuals

appeared to love enduring fellowships more than they do in present day times when the electronic world moves quick and regularly continues on leaving juvenile connections that didn't get the opportunity to create. Syb observed Uncle Sam's accounts intriguing; I thought that they are enthralling and contacting.

During Uncle Sam's somewhat meandering memory of the sort individuals who so heartily accepted the RAF cadets during their preparation at Falcon Field, he halted and took a gander at Syb. My little girl did not know what was on the old kid's psyche.

"My Mesa family had a girl who was about your age, Syb," Uncle Sam said. "Furthermore, think about what; she was the person who sewed my wings on in the wake of preparing – since my mom and sisters were great many miles away."

s we had effectively learned, Uncle Sam was an admirer of old vehicles which was highlighted while he prepared at Falcon Field in Mesa which is the place where he purchased the Cadillac LaSalle roadster that he nicknamed the "Yellow Pearl." Connecting those some time in the past days with the wedding that would be occurring that day, Jez and Sarah would show up at the wedding sanctuary in the Yellow Pearl. Uncle Sam by then had the laser-like focus of my girl and inquired as to whether Syb might want to see the Yellow Pearl. Obviously she was unable to say no!

As we strolled to the carport where the Yellow Pearl was kept, Sam snatched a stick; I saw that he had a perceptible limp. The subject of how he was harmed streaked momentarily through my psyche. He just sloughed it off as an old physical issue without being explicit. Syb adored the old vehicle; she spouted about it such a lot of that Uncle Sam proposed to give it to her. Obviously, coordinations wouldn't take into consideration that, yet I was moved by the liberal deal.

With our visit at its end, Syb and I bid farewell to Uncle Sam, expressed gratitude toward him for his accounts and friendliness. I saw a hint of misery in Uncle Sam's eyes. I realized he was pondering when he'd have the option to share his memories of those wonder days once more. However, it was the ideal opportunity for us to leave his organization and turn our concentration back to the first reason for our outing – the wedding where we'd get together with him once more.

Just as in US culture, the Brits embraced the practice of the lady of the hour wearing "something old, a novel, new thing, something acquired and something blue" during the wedding service – as images of best of luck for the couple's future. The custom really started in an Old English rhyme. As a lady, Sarah had an exceptionally strange "something old" that she would be wearing on her big day as a rabbit's foot.

* *

fter the wedding service, Syb and I were praising the glad couple who remained with the wedding part in the gathering line. I hadn't seen Sarah in seemingly forever. We embraced and traded welcomes and great wishes and I gladly acquainted her with my girl. I could see the delight in Sarah's eyes. After a nearby and suffering relationship with Jez, she had at long last turned into his better half. Syb's eyes quickly went to the RAF wings that were sewn close to the scooped neck of Sarah's delightful outfit. It was Uncle Sam's RAF wings. Sarah quickly saw Syb's advantage in them.

"Uncle Sam let me acquire his RAF wings from World War II for best of luck. Isn't so great?!"

"He should truly like you since he's so glad for them. He showed them to us yesterday!" Syb reacted.

I feel respected," Sarah reacted. "He permitted me to get the image of a period in his life that holds such a lot of significance for him."

"I'm certain that Uncle Sam's wings will carry an exceptional gift to your marriage," Syb told Sarah.

I was pleased with Syb. She got it – she got Uncle Sam and she got how significant that great period had been to him.

As we strolled on, we observed Uncle Sam toward the finish of the gathering line. He had a little heap of envelopes, yellowed with age and attached with a radiant red strip. He grinned broadly as Syb approached him.

"I tracked down the letters – the adoration letters from the young lady in Mesa – you realize the person who looked actually like you," Uncle Sam said.

Syb was understanding and grinned as she tenderly took the heap of letters from a very long time before that Uncle Sam gave her.

"I'd like you to have them. You wouldn't fret an elderly person living in the beyond a bit, do you youngster?" Uncle Sam asked detecting that he might be irritating Syb.

"obviously not, Uncle Sam," Syb told him. "I'll peruse your letters and relish each word. It's a little cut of the historical backdrop of both our nations."

yb's words carried a couple of tears to the elderly person's eyes.

What a thoughtful young lady my girl was. I had until recently never been more pleased with her.

The RAF Cadets of Falcon Field

A fter the wedding, our encounter with Uncle Sam waited to me. I had partaken in the entirety of his accounts and imagined how it more likely than not been for himself and other youthful RAF cadets to go to the United States for cutting edge preparing. Obviously, it was a quill in our country's cap that the Brits accepted our pilot preparing focuses to be better than their own. I was delighted to hear that the nearby individuals greeted them wholeheartedly. The experience that the British pilots had was an ideal illustration of what's truly going on with America. It made me proud.

Other visitors at the wedding helped me to remember the penances that were made for the benefit of opportunity during World War II. At the gathering following the wedding, we sat almost an older refined man wearing a Scottish kilt and decorations, flagging the valorous commitment that little nations like Scotland and Ireland and apparently unbiased nations like those in Scandinavia made secretively that aided lead to triumph over Nazism. This man of honor found a seat at our table. He didn't talk except if addressed. I felt he accepted the awards he bore on his chest did his talking for him. As far as I might be concerned, they did. The distant examine his eyes was like that of Uncle Sam's the point at which he talked about the conflict years. At the point when the expression, "You must be there... " is spoken – it very well may be not any more relevant than portraying the encounters of these men who battled and endure the biggest and most lethal conflict ever.

was interested and moved by Uncle Sam's story. The sparkle in his eye when he talked of procuring his wings also enduring an extremely intense preparing program was a picture that remained with me. I concluded I needed to more deeply study the RAF pilots at Thunderbird. Maybe the phantoms of those youthful cadets were calling to me to recount their story. At the point when I got back to the States after the wedding, not set in stone to dive in and track down all that I

could about them.

I got more familiar with Uncle Sam whose complete name was Samuel Charles Waddington. While in the RAF he rose to the position of Flight Lieutenant and was shot somewhere around the Germans when he was the co-pilot of a Lancaster plane on a strike on Berlin. Lieutenant Waddington was harmed in the accident and went through a year in a German POW camp. Those were subtleties that Uncle Sam neglected to tell us. He told us of his happiness flying and of battling for and guarding his country. Like most fighters who have battled in wars, it is frequently too agonizing to even consider reviewing the dull days of their experience. I had more regard and honor for Uncle Sam than any time in recent memory subsequent to learning of the full-broadness of his administration. The wellspring of the "old injury" that caused Uncle Sam's super durable limp was currently clarified.

PT-17 cadet tying on his parachute

During my examination, one of the main things I learned was the RAF needed to take no less than a similarity to responsibility for preparing program. They were allocated to what exactly Jack Connelly, one of the authors of Southwest Airlines, had wanted to name Thunderbird Field III yet the Brits recoiled. To

them, the name "Thunderbird" was weird sounding and held no significance for them. The Brits squeezed the Southwest leaders to change the name to something more OK, had more importance for themselves and could be straightforwardly related to them. To carry the nearby inhabitants in with the general mish-mash, the base requested name ideas from the local area that would need to acknowledge another name also. Somebody proposed that the field be renamed Falcon Field which evidently satisfied everybody with the conceivable special case of Jack Connelly who was not exactly excited. In any case, eventually to stay away from a roundabout contention about the name of the field, Falcon Field acquired Connelly's imprimatur, Connelly was centered around the more significant matter of building up the field and starting the preparation. The immediate connection to Great Britain was the hawk, a flying predator that had solid prominence in England. Maybe it was a picture that evoked strength against the mistreatment that Europe, including Great Britain, was battling against.

The initial four classes of British cadets showed up via train from Canada. The young fellows were all wearing indistinguishable official dim non military personnel suits and conveying indistinguishable official earthy colored cardboard bags. They had not yet procured their "wings" so they were not given the standard military pack sacks. It was during the Roosevelt organization which was attempting to make light of US nonpartisanship in the conflict that was starting to devour Europe.

I started to burrow for data about the RAF cadets at Falcon Field on the Internet. At first, I figured it very well may be difficult to track down a lot. Man was I off-base! I read the memories of an old British gent who had been one of the cadets. He composed that on his appearance to Falcon Field with different cadets in his gathering the temperature was a rankling 100+ degrees – something that simply doesn't happen in the UK. The cadets were met by the Cadet Officer of the Day, evidently the pilot learner who performed especially well that day. The youngsters' mouths were watering for a reviving cold brew however rather were quickly prompted the preparation field for a series of workout! They thought they were done following an hour of hopping jacks, side ride jumps, push-ups and sit-ups yet were let the awful news know that there would be more – they needed to hurry to the far fence and back. Also, clearly the "far fence" was extremely "far." Most of the youngsters were in great state of being nevertheless the fence was a pretty far. What's more, with the temperature more than 100 degrees, the mile appeared to be more similar to five miles to the depleted and baffled young fellows. The mile run and back assumed control over a half-hour. A portion of the cadets didn't return until it was past seven o'clock that evening. The main positive thing that

could be credited to the late return was that the temperature had dropped to a "cool" 95!

PT-17 arrangement flying.

obviously US cadet pilots at the Thunderbird preparing offices far dwarfed unfamiliar students including the Brits. There was a well disposed competition between the US and pilots from different countries yet especially with the British cadets. The instructional meetings were directed independently in light of the fact that there were slight contrasts in their projects. While American preparing focused on accuracy flying, Chandelles, Lazy Eights, Pylon Turns and short field arrivals, the British focused on other flying abilities. It was a generally expected saying among the Americans at Thunderbird that any arrival was viewed as a decent one when you left a decent landing! The Brits were obviously more worried about wonderful three-point arrivals.

The greatest inquiry I needed to find a response for was the reason the British chose to send their cadets to the US, explicitly to Falcon Field, for their preparation. In the wake of burrowing, I discovered that in 1940 the Brits were encountering vexing issues with the preparation of their new pilots. There were a few factors that added to the circumstance. The English climate was not solid

for preparing new fliers. "Hazy London town" was not simply an idiom. There was additionally an issue of geology. Britain isn't colossal in region and there simply weren't sufficient appropriate fields on which to prepare the men. Added to those basic issues, the Brits were lacking in planes and on fuel denying the RAF to build up a preparation program sufficiently sufficient to get ready youthful pilots for the genuine fight noticeable all around that was turning out to be progressively approaching. A lacking preparing project or office just wouldn't do.

There was not such an extravagance as time in 1940. The Germans were acquiring power and region in Europe and the danger to Great Britain was undeniable. To facilitate the preparation of their cadets in a program that would deliver the best RAF pilots in the most speedy manner conceivable, they concocted the "Domain Air Training Scheme." With the arrangement of other unified countries, the arrangement would send youthful Brits to unfamiliar terrains to accept their essential and progressed preparing programs. The first arrangement incorporated the countries of Canada, South Africa and Rhodesia. Nonetheless, subsequent to asking for help from the American government, the US was added to the record.

RAF Squadron Leader Stuart Mills was dispatched to the United States to help with setting up the fields for the projected preparing program and to guarantee that needs that the Brits had set up for their pilots would be met. The arrangement among America and Great Britain required the US to commit six fields for RAF pilot preparing, one of which was probably intended to be in Mesa, Arizona. Also, that was the field that would ultimately be renamed from Thunderbird III Field to Falcon Field .

Mills came to Falcon Field straightforwardly from the front line; he had taken on in the lamentable Conflict of Norway. His group was named the Glosser Gladiators and it had been working in regrettable conditions that were situated in a frozen lake where he had been injured. The group was being crushed and needed to escape, abandoning all airplane. At the point when Mills got word that he was being requested to the US, he had no clue the reason and why it had been he who was chosen for the obscure task. However, he was recuperating from rout and injury and going to the US would take him off the combat zone and the opportunity for a total recuperation so he could serve once more. As he headed out to the US, he just had requests to answer to the British Embassy in Washington, DC. He'd discover then the "why" part of the task.

Mills might have met his entry on the troopship, Empress of Britain, with a touch of humor. He was appointed to the "special night" suite with a British

radar master. The lodge was confined and loaded up with containers of reconnaissance gear that at last ended up in Hawaii. Regardless of whether the special night suite had been utilized for a recently hitched couple the condition of the lodge would not have been helpful for sentiment. Somewhat fun during wartime ought to be viewed as the genuine meaning of "lighthearted element."

Mills had the opportunity to rest during the journey to assist with mending his injury and to attempt to let recollections of the fight and the pictures of his dead and harmed friends behind him. Obviously, recollections like those are rarely really abandoned. However, he had a new thing to zero in on – he didn't have a clue what yet it would be new. After first showing up in Halifax, Nova Scotia, Mills ventured out to Washington, DC, to realize what was coming up for him. He was amazed when he was welcome to the White House for tea with the Roosevelts – obviously an absolutely surprising occasion. It appeared FDR and his counselors needed to address him to get a direct interpretation of the Battle of Norway and overall with regards to the conflict currently seething in Europe. The Americans weren't in the conflict by then yet were sufficiently shrewd to realize that they would be involved one day and presumably not long from now.

Finally, after tea in the early evening, Mills was told by British commandants what his task in the US would be. He was given the obligation of choosing landing strips and directing the preparation of British RAF cadets in the United States. He would traverse the huge country and investigate the foundation of preparing fields in California, Texas, Oklahoma and Florida and, obviously, Mesa, Arizona, where the unbelievable Falcon Field would at last be in activity.

Mills arrived at Phoenix's Sky Harbor Airport to assess the chances in Arizona for a high level instructional hub for RAF cadets. He was met by Jack Connelly, Leland Hayward and Al Storrs who were the authors of Southwest Airlines and were associated with building up preparing fields for Americans just as unfamiliar pilots. It was war time – time to get down to business – and large number of pilots should have been prepared. Al Storrs eventually was made head of preparing at Falcon Field. After a couple of merriments, the men took the youthful British official to the proposed area for the RAF preparing field.

t the hour of Southwest Airways' cooperation in aiding the determination and foundation of pilot preparing fields in the United States, the organization was simply in its youngster arranges and wasn't anyplace close to the stalwart that it at last became. Southwest began with Thunderbird I then, at that point, developed to incorporate Thunderbird II, Sky Harbor and Falcon Field.

Mills stayed befuddled and unsure during the excursion to the proposed preparing office. They traveled numerous miles down a dusty street during which Mills was in a close to condition of shock when they adjusted a bend and passed a Native American on a pony, towing a transporter with a child inside – the child's mom running close by the transporter so she could watch out for the child. Factories had never seen such a sight having lived in sprightly old England his whole life. The others chuckled at his response. It was as yet normal in Arizona around then to see the nearby Native Americans riding a horse and living as numerous ages of their kin had lived for a really long time. However, given Mills previously befuddled state and the shock of seeing something he had presumably just found in the films, he needed to imagine that the American West was to be sure still the Wild West!

Plants couldn't have been promptly intrigued with the parcel of land that Connelly and the others showed him. It was simply dry desolate desert! The main items other than unending sand were an immense orange woods where the ground level rose strongly and on the north side of the field a gigantic level beat mountain that could be seen off not too far off.

ills rushed to make an evaluation. He concluded that the orange forest would need to be moved back and that the key position would need to be evened out off. He normally was thinking as far as runways and departures. Since Southwest was taking on a portion of the monetary weight and hazard, Connelly and the others were worried about his ideas and remarks. The modifications that Mills was suggesting would be expensive. Southwest was frustrated for cash at that point and Mills' proposed changes would require more cash than they had accessible.

ills attempted to streamline the other men's interests with a little British humor.

"One thing we will not need to do is move the mountain."

"There is a God," Connelly reacted with a fake moan of alleviation.

The others concurred that it was uplifting news. As it ended up, it wasn't important to move or reduction the orange woods. Indeed, the forest actually stands today creating natural product like it had been accomplishing for a really long time. The ground didn't need to be evened out all things considered. They had the option to get a good deal on those exorbitant changes by planning the arrangement of the proposed field around those future obstructions. Not adjusting the land, the expense of the field didn't burn through every last cent, yet those administering the undertaking ensured that it was alright for the new cadets who might be preparing there.

Things didn't go totally flawlessly after Mills at first consented to the real estate parcel for the instructional hub. He was dubious with regards to Southwest's capacity to convey the high level instructional hub that he imagined. Subsequent to talking with them and riddling them with questions, he inferred that they had practically zero experience working "Harvards" or running an enormous preparing base. Thunderbird Field was pristine and quite a bit of Southwest's assets had been exhausted in the structure and foundation of the field. On the positive side, Mills was intrigued with the climate. The calm environment and predominantly clear skies were ideal for the preparation of new pilots. As it turned out the warm, dry environment of that area of Arizona credited to the general achievement of Thunderbird and the preparation activity.

PT-17 nightfall 2-transport

After Mills gave his last blessing on Falcon Field, development started right away. The starting of flying tasks trailed on September 14, 1941, even amidst the disarray and vulnerability of new development. At the point when the principal RAF cadets came through for preparing the runway, sleeping quarters and helper offices were not completely finished or

prepared however time was of the quintessence. The conflict and propelling Nazism wouldn't stand by. The cadets figured out how to drink milk as opposed to relying upon the untrustworthy water that when it sputtered out of the tap streamed out a light corroded orange. Heaps of timber around the site drew an amazing number of crickets. The creepy crawlies apparently stacked up toward the edges of the shelter four or five inches down. Their evening time ensemble made dozing hard for the depleted cadets who required rest for the thorough preparing necessities. A gathering of British cadets were scared when they recognized an enormous rattler that had steered up close to the shelter. It was a picture previously unheard of by the youthful pilots. The incredible climate was fairly tempered by the presence of bugs and reptiles.

In request to permit the RAF cadets the whole day for preparing moves, all the standard support of the planes, gear and runway were done around evening time. Every night the unending round of fixes and safeguard upkeep on the planes started – valve changing, plug changing, oil changes, brake checks, tire fixes or substitutions and harm fix – all to guarantee that the cadets would prepare on protected, very much kept up with planes every morning. Ladies were a significant piece of the evening upkeep group. They were essentially utilized for lubing the tail wheel orientation and tail gear toss out grips. Primary concern, numerous long periods of additional time and twofold time were piled up by the support group and staff.

As preparing proceeded, there were a couple "knocks" along the landing area way. While the Brits were content with the security norms and upkeep plan, they were less happy with the preparation program itself. They scrutinized the proficiency of essential, fundamental and progressed flight preparing. The British aeronautics specialists scrutinized the need of the essential piece of the program. They likewise didn't care for the Vultee BT-13 airplanes which was utilized in preparing drills.

The Brits viewed the Vultee as hard to keep up with and noticed central underlying imperfections which were eventually remedied. In the courses wherein the Vultee was utilized, time was lost when up to half of the class was grounded in view of the Vultee's imperfections.

Shadows in the Sand" photograph by Ray Shelton

In the end the Brits won the day. After a brief time frame in the wake of preparing started, the fundamental preparing segment was disposed of for RAF cadets and afterward started their preparation in what had been the optional or essential portion of the US program.

Another distinction that emerged with the British learners was comparative with late evening flying tasks which were essential for the essential part of the American program. Solo night arrivals on a 450 x 100 yard flare-way was needed at the midpoint in starting preparing. It was an issue since the RAF cadets needed to figure out how to take-off, fly and land around evening time – a time when numerous forays would be led in genuine battle. The British at first utilized Thunderbird Field with flare pots set up to check the watered down runway for night flight preparing until Falcon was finished. The strip was kept watered down to hold the sand back from cleaning up on departure and landing.

I perceived that the RAF cadets who were in preparing at Falcon Field needed to have had an entirely unexpected attitude than the Americans who were preparing there. At the point when the principal cadets came to Arizona, it was before the Pearl Harbor assault and the United States was, obviously, still actually nonpartisan. At first, the cadets were told to wear easygoing non military personnel garments. Yet, England was at war and was being assaulted. The cadets should have been in uniform – there was nothing relaxed with regards to war! Hence, relaxed clothing was absolutely improper to Mills and the other British officials with whom he had contact.

Stuart Mills instinctually realized that the preparation could not the slightest bit be viewed as everything except earnest and genuine. He understood that discipline would be close to outlandish except if the British cadets were needed to wear their regalia. It would be a consistent token of why they were there, how genuine their preparation was and what confronted them when they got back to England. He presented his defense to the American preparing staff and despite the fact that it was against standard working systems because of America's present noninterventionist strategy and the restricting of military regalia at preparing focuses, the Americans submitted.

Despite conflicts and the two sides making concessions and changes, to an English, Scottish or Welsh youth who had been chosen for the US flight preparing program in far off Arizona, a large portion of a world away, it was high experience. By and large, away from their British homes for almost nine months. At the point when they got back, they would confront functional preparing in their locally situated preparing fields lastly the genuine article – real battle. The youngsters had taken on a significant obligation and possible risk in joining to shield their country. I respected these fearless youngsters significantly more subsequent to finding out with regards to their encounters.

The 13 Black Cats

A s Lianne and I were driving across the American Legion extension, only north of Washington DC, Lianne says "South Ops today, father!" as she focuses to the fly plane overhead. "I believe it's an American Airlines 737... that's right, two motors under the wing, red, white and blue tail and winglets as well!" Lianne and I have been playing this game for a long time and she is getting very great at recognizing the kind of plane, carriage and the land direction at Washington Reagan National Airport or DCA.

"How about we play another game today" I say to Lianne. She's as of now doing some variable based math and trig, so a few divisions ought to be simple for this shrewd young lady. "Alright, I say, if that 737 over overflies the American Legion Bridge at 3,000' and 10 nautical miles (NM) away from landing and is on a 3 degree coast way, at what stature will the 73 be at 5 nautical miles?"

"Father , truly?"

"Goodness come on, consider it. I'll give you a clue. Pilots allude to it as the 3 to 1 guideline". I say with a difficult smile.

"Alright, I'll check it out" says Lianne as she starts thinking critically. "In the event that a 737 is at 3,000' at 10 miles, at 1,500' it ought to be at... midway or 5 miles!" she yells.

We proceed with our drive south bound on the George Washington Parkway as we follow the flight way of a few planes arranging themselves for arriving at DCA on runway 19. I tell Lianne, "I've flown this appearance many occasions in my profession and it never goes downhill. It is presumably the most difficult and fun appearance into any air terminal in the United States. "Pilots are needed to follow the tight Potomac River right to arriving to keep away from structures and a few secure regions along the course to incorporate the CIA, Vice President house and regions close to the White House." I trill as Lianne scarcely is by all accounts paying

consideration.

Alright Lianne, another piece of random data. How tall is the Washington Monument?" as we drive by the National Capital's most unmistakable milestone.

No thought,

father" she says. I

say " it's 555 feet"

Lianne gazes upward and sees a plane overhead, abeam the landmark and making its last go to arrive on runway 19 at DCA. She proclaims spontaneous, "Two Miles!! We're two miles from the air terminal on the off chance that the fly is at a similar stature as the Washington Monument!"

he is correct and I contemplate internally that I've been raising a flying virtuoso. Be that as it may, I've recounted to the story multiple times to any individual who might tune in. Once upon a time, I was instructed by an old hard 727 Captain that when you're were close to the Washington Monument or approx. 600 feet and two miles out, you ought to be very near a 3 degree skim way to arrive on runway 19 in DCA.

Today, Lianne is making a trip with me to Dallas Ft. Worth (DFW) International Airport, however not so much for any pleasant delays this time. Today, I'm booked for a test system meeting in the Boeing 777-200 at the American Airlines preparing focus only south of the air terminal. I'll be at the instructional hub for a large portion of a day, to incorporate briefings and the test system and Lianne gets an opportunity to have a long lunch with some family.

As we get off the plane at entryway D24, Lianne and I are welcomed by my Aunt Marilyn, who is an airline steward with American Airlines. She is simply getting off a homegrown excursion and is anticipating taking Lianne out somewhere else. The two will meet my Uncle Mike who is a resigned business carrier pilot living in North Texas.

As a child growing up, my Uncle Mike was my legend. He soloed at 15 years of age, had his private permit at 16 years and proceeded to turn into a teacher a couple of years after the fact. Uncle Mike's educator was his father, my granddad, Leo Purinton. Like Uncle Mike, my Aunt Marilyn is likewise a pilot with an instrument rating and verged on seeking after her business pilot's permit, yet chose being an airline steward was a superior fit for her way of life and her land business.

Lianne, Marilyn and Mike all plunk down for lunch at a Lewisville BBQ cafe, when Lianne asks all of a sudden, "Inform me concerning your Uncle Jimmy"

ike begins the discussion first, " My uncle and your Great Uncle 'Jimmy' Purinton was a pilot at Thunderbird Field close to Phoenix, Arizona

way back in 1941"

" I accept he was brought into the world in Superior, Nebraska, in 1906 and first became keen on zooming around 1926. So that made him four years more established than my father."

Marilyn puts down her espresso and says."My father used to recount to me the story, that his more established sibling, Jimmy began by assisting a nearby pilot with the circumstance on a magneto on his plane motor." She proceeds. "It was generally new to Uncle Jimmy yet he appeared to have an inborn skill for anything aeronautical. Maybe there was a DNA strand that was contained the 'flying' quality that was passed for in a real sense ages."

Mike ringed in "And I was one of the fortunate beneficiaries of their adoration for flying." Mike tells Lianne, "I had a 40+ year profession in flight and I can thank my Uncle Jimmy and father for that."

Marilyn rushed to note "Uncle Jimmy's ability for this new industry that was clearing the country and astounding the world. As an extremely young fellow he was extended to an employment opportunity with the Rola Radio Company that was, at that point, one of the debut tech organizations exploring different avenues regarding airplane radio frameworks." Lianne was shockingly still drawn in and added. "Sounds good to me! – Anyone flying noticeable all around, surely required a method for conversing with individuals on the ground and air."

CAA authentication for Cleo Glenn "Jimmy" Purinton....#4951

Mike, who is a genuine understudy of flight added. "In the same way as other different businesses, the flight business generated until recently never envisioned ventures like airplane radio. Avionics had a worldwide effect that changed the manner in which we lived and worked together – and transformed it until the end of time. The Internet made the world more modest yet one might say avionics made the world bigger with more freedoms for everybody from common men to corporate monsters. Uncle Jimmy was offered a compensation in addition to the guarantee of flying examples. In spite of the fact that he wouldn't concede to this is on the grounds that he wanted the cash, the flying illustrations were more critical to Jimmy than his compensation was. He, obviously, acknowledged the proposition, turned into an authorized pilot and fled of his grown-up life."

Marilyn proceeds to share a story, "I coincidentally found Uncle Jimmy's pilot permit in a case with my father's avionics things and found that his CAA pilot's authentication was the number 4951."

ianne inquired, "What's the significance here?"

Marilyn proceeds to say, "As a method for portraying Uncle Jimmy's place in flying history, let me give a couple of names and numbers that will be edifying you. Orville Wright was one!... Wilbur Wright was two!"

"And my Great Uncle Jimmy Purinton was number 4951!!!" says Lianne with fervor.

"Yes!" says both Marilyn and Mike as one.

Mike takes a taste of his ice tea and is astounded to see he actually has Lianne's complete consideration. "Allow me to recount to you one more anecdote about Uncle Jimmy that almost cost him his life!"

Lianne's eyes are totally open now as she listens eagerly.

Thunderbird Instructor arm band given to Jimmy Purinton with US pilot no. 4951

Mike begins, "Thinking back to the 1940's, the PT-17 or Stearman airplane had no radios and accordingly there was no sound association with ground control. At the point when a cadet or understudy pilot entered the traffic example to land or do "contact and goes" he was working rigorously on visuals for sure was alluded to as a "see and keep away from" premise. It's not hard to comprehend the disarray and even turmoil that likely existed while envisioning in a real sense many airplanes in exceptionally bustling rush hour gridlock designs attempting to keep away from each other as they played out their training drills."

He proceeds, "Intermittently teachers would remain on the ground and holler directions to their understudies who could possibly get a couple of words from 500' to 1,000' above. Different occasions the teacher would hop into his own Stearman coach and either lead or follow his understudy in the rush hour gridlock design and have the option to "educate" from the air versus the ground."

He proceeds to say, "Obviously, regardless it was anything but an exceptionally protected or dependable activity and it was one that welcomed calamity and fiasco is the thing that nearly happened on 15 September 1943. On that day, Cadets Pfeffer and Gadd were performing contact and goes in the rush hour gridlock design yet neglected to focus on their teacher and ended up landing directly on top of Jimmy who was perched on the landing area in his PT-17. As anyone might expect, the occurrence totally annihilated Uncle Jimmy's plane and harmed the airplane the cadets were flying. It didn't be anything under a sheer wonder that nobody was killed or significantly harmed."

"Goodness" says Lianne, "Uncle Jimmy might have been killed!"

Marilyn adds, "I recollect that story being told when I was close to nothing. Uncle Jimmy supported minor wounds to his head and shoulder yet made a full recuperation. Furthermore, was back flying only a couple of days after the fact."

Lianne, with lunch got done, just arranged her cherished pastry of frozen yogurt and chocolate sauce. at the point when Marilyn hauled something out of her handbag.

It was an old news story dated October 16, 1964 from the Times of Rouge River, Oregon.

Marilyn shows Lianne the article and sums up.

Jimmy Purinton worked with a significant number of the 13 Black Cats travelers on films set in Southern California.

"Jimmy was refered to as thinking back with regards to how 35 years before he had partaken in the commitment of another landing strip in Medford, he guided the principal business plane out of Medford; his travelers were the Mayor of Medford and his better half. On one significant flight, he conveyed a daily existence saving serum to a medical clinic that was treating a young fellow experiencing meningitis. The article covered different parts of his profession. Perusers without a doubt thought that it is intriguing to discover that Jimmy was associated with the 13 Black Cats trouping bunch just as early avionics themed films.

He additionally flew heavyweight champion Jack Dempsey and other Hollywood illuminators like Wallace Beery, Jean Harlow and Helen Twelvetrees on private sanctioned flights. Jimmy worked north of seven years in the motion pictures and participated in milestone movies, for example, Wings which featured Clara Bow and Gary Cooper. He performed aeronautical tricks in motion pictures including Lilac Time, Test Pilot and Hell's Angels. He additionally assumed a part in Men with Wings which was a Walt Disney creation. He was likewise in various shorts. Jimmy was incredible among the youngsters of his old neighborhood.

Hollywood Aviation films with Jimmy
Purinton as a flying
extra

Two little fellows had saved their pennies to pay for a ride on a plane guided by Jimmy. One of the young men bragged about Jimmy's ideal three-point landing, asserting that no pilot could outperform

Jimmy's flying capacities. After

serving a deployment at Pearl Harbor during World War II, Jimmy turned into an educator at Thunderbird Field."

Again Lianne says, "Goodness! Uncle Jimmy truly was a piece of flying history."

"I have one final fast story," says Mike. "Then, at that point, we need to return you once again to the air terminal and meet your father for your trip back."

Lianne looks somewhat baffled yet begins to lick the lower part of her frozen yogurt bowl.

Mike starts, "Do you recollect the tale of Sully and the Miracle on the Hudson?"

Lianne says,"Yes we headed out to see that film the year before."

"Indeed, Uncle Jimmy completed a "marvel" arrival of his own. He had motor disappointment similar to Sully. What's more, he had to set down the plane he was flying in a furrowed field in the wake of spiraling down from a height of 2,000 feet. He was not harmed yet his plane experienced significant harm when it hit the delicate soil and went end over end for a long time before it fell in a store. My Uncle Jimmy Purinton returned seven days after the fact to his flight educator obligations and was living confirmation that you can't hold a decent pilot down, and verification that our family would stay dedicated to flying regardless difficulties they were facing or the risk that was innate chasing their enthusiasm for taking off into the mists."

Jimmy Puriton and companion "Boots" with the 13 Black Cat Model T Ford

"Check please!" says Mike. As he waves a mark motion.

The Daughter of Thunderbird Field

My dad has been a painter all his life. It started when he was at San Jose State University and it continues today as he leads watercolor classes near Santa Fe, NM. This weekend he is in Southern Colorado with a gathering of six understudies and my mother gets an uncommon opportunity to come visit us in Washington D.C.

After I get my mother at the air terminal we start to talk "You realize I've been exploring your Dad's, Leo Purinton, flying memorabilia for the beyond couple of months and I've never truly gotten an opportunity to get some information about what you recollect. How old would you say you were the point at which you were at Thunderbird? What do you recollect that?" I inquired. "Would you be able to enlighten me concerning your experience?"

y mother looks somewhat astonished by my inquiries, but on the other hand she's glad to tell her child a portion of the family ancestry, thus she starts to fill me in regarding it. "I'm an offspring of Thunderbird Field as my father, Leo Purinton, was a flight educator there from 1942 to 1944. I was brought into the world in Klamath Falls, Oregon in 1932. At 5 years old years old, I lost my mom. It was amidst the downturn so things were very agitated for a serious time. My grandma lived with us while my father, Leo, worked for an organization called Weyerhauser Lumber in Oregon."

Alyce Purinton. "Attendant" with Pan America. Around 1954

"Was it hard on you? the family?" I request that as I proceed with drive.

Life was a battle to meet finishes. My father worked 50-60 hours out of each week to help his family and went through any extra cash he had getting aeronautics licenses in Klamath Falls, Oregon. He'd commonly fly on the ends of the week when not at work and typically his flights were close to 15 minutes all at once. This was everything he could manage. It took my father north of 8 years just to accept his private pilot's permit. However, it showed me at an early age the significance of commitment and being energetic for something you really love." Says my mother.

Then she proceeds. " Shortly after the demise of my mom, we moved to the Bay Area (Oakland, California), remaining with different relatives. This was because of the demise of my mom, the Depression, and the drawing closer

World War II. As a youngster growing up and even as a grown-up, I never truly felt appended to wherever until my significant other, RC "Doc" Weaver and I resigned and moved to Santa Fe, New Mexico. Doc's experience is pretty much something very similar." Mom is truly getting into a cadence now, thus she proceeds with her story… our story. "At the point when we were residing in Oakland California region, where Dad was training for Civil Air Patrol, is the point at which his more established sibling, Jimmy Purinton, called him about educator openings at Thunderbird Field in Glendale, Arizona. He considered this to be an extraordinary chance to serve, bring in a minimal expenditure and furthermore to proceed with his energy for flying. While he went to Thunderbird Field to get gotten comfortable, I remained behind with my grandma in Vancouver, Wash."

"This was wartime and everybody contributed. My grandma was working in a shipyard there and Dad was preparing pilots in Phoenix (Glendale). Everybody was associated with the safeguard and backing of our nation and partners. Indeed, even at such a youthful age I could feel the nation meeting up for one reason, I may have not perceived the specific explanation, yet I realized it was significant."

The voice of my mom trails off as she expresses these words to me, as she stays silent for a brief period. Furthermore, as I'm staying there driving, I attempt to envision what regular day to day existence resembled in those days, and how a kid might actually comprehend all that was happening at that point.

y mother ends the quiet and brings me back from my considerations as she continues with the story. "While residing in Washington, I went to a one room school out in the nation where I was even permitted to avoid a grade. It was around then my Dad sent for myself and I took my first business flight and flew from Portland, Oregon to Phoenix, Arizona. My father had tracked down a little spot to live in Glendale which currently has been wrapped by Phoenix. I accept the town of Phoenix was uniquely around 100.000 individuals then, at that point, and Glendale a lot more modest and out in the desert."

She proceeds, "While at Thunderbird Field my Dad for the most part showed American cadets in the PT-17 (Stearman) and they regularly went to the house on ends of the week. One of his first cadets was a young fellow by the name of Bill Poore who later came to work for Dad in his flight activities after the conflict as a teacher in Montague, Ca and afterward and Redding, Ca."

Mom laughs a bit and I get some information about, she continues and tells me, "One of my beloved recollections was of my Dad and his Chinese cadets. They were extremely youthful, as every one of the cadets were, and exceptionally pleasant. They

called me May Ling, as that was Mrs. Chiang Kai Check's name, and they venerated her. At age 10 they would take me to Glendale's midtown pharmacy wellspring, where they would arrange rehashed rounds of Coke for us. This satisfied me enormously on the grounds that I was once in a while permitted Coke at home.

My father, your grandpa, was a solitary parent, in no place, in World War II when he met and wedded his second spouse Dorothea Rexroad. However, it didn't work out and they separated, perhaps eighteen months after, I think, my father assisted her with getting her pilot's permit, and she later proceeded to fly as a pilot in the Women Air Force Service Pilots (WASP). Since my father was flying such a huge amount at that point, it was then that I was sent back to my grandmas. Some way or another, I don't recall precisely, Dad was drafted into the military towards the finish of the conflict. His agreement was fulfilled at Thunderbird. He left Glendale and was delivered out to a Texas armed force base and was subsequently delivered as the conflict finished. He returned to Klamath Falls, Oregon where he met his prospective, third spouse, Marie, who was showing school there."

"Did grandpa at any point need to fly for any business carrier?" I inquire.

Mom shakes her head as she answers. "My father adored flying, wasn't keen on flying for Pan American or Trans World Airways (TWA), however at that point he knew about a requirement for a decent base administrator (FBO) in Northern California in Montague. Due to his experience as a flight teacher at Thunderbird, he took over training every one of the veterans in the space utilizing the recently shaped Federal ordered G I Bill, and others obviously. He additionally turned into a vendor for Piper Aircraft, selling little airplane for the upstart organization. He and Marie were hitched, and I went to secondary school in neighboring Yreka, California. Marie educated there until her three youngsters (Marilyn, Mike and Patty) were conceived.

My Dad consistently flew sanctions, in light of the fact that Yreka was very remote. He additionally worked for the woods administration each late spring flying individuals, freight, and so on In this piece of the United States, where the summers are sweltering and dry, there were bunches of timberland fires in the wild regions. My father really cherished flying with the backwoods administration, in light of the fact that each flight was unique and they were continually attempting to track down better approaches to help the immense exertion of battling timberland fires. Aeronautics and woodland fires avoidance was another exchange at that point and he cherished being on the ground floor. He recounted to me the story how he lost a motor in the Marble Mountains and had a constrained arriving upon the mountain. The plane arrived at slow speed, possibly 50 mph, hit a tree and flipped over on its top. He left with just minor cuts and injuries. He needed to stroll down to the

firemen and brave a pony. Right up 'til the present time, the airplane is still up there." "Goodness, I never realized that ! That is a remarkable story!" I shout. "Shouldn't something be said about you and father? Why you didn't work an aeronautics work ?" I keep on asking as we maneuver into the carport.

"I sure did!" answers my mother. " But it's been a drawn out day, so let me subside into my "relative" suite in the cellar and I'll let you know the rest. Ensure you hang tight for me with a glass of white wine, please" she says with a wink as she heads to her space for a brief reprieve.

After a short time, she comes up the steps and sits down on the lounge chair so we can proceed with our discussion about family flying history. She is by all accounts truly having fun, and I'm glad we are having this opportunity to reconnect and discuss Leo.

"So you were informing me regarding your flying profession, mother... "

My mother gestures and keeps on telling me in the wake of taking a taste from her glass of wine. "I graduated in 1949 and went to San Jose State University. I studied Business Administration/Marketing and had minored in Spanish. After school I filled in as a purchaser learner for an enormous San Francisco retail chain called The Emporium. I could have done without my after-school profession, and a man from Pan Am came to San Francisco talking with Spanish speakers for their Latin American Division. I was recruited on the spot and traveled to Miami with 4 different Californians through Mexico City and Havana. We prepared at Pan Am's middle in Miami and were shipped off New York to travel to the Caribbean Islands, Venezuela, Brazil, Uruguay and Argentina. Flying was substantially more socialized back then. We didn't have five star, since it was generally top notch. Spanish was fundamental and, when in Brazil, local people saw sufficient Spanish for us to be perceived. Skillet Am's other aircraft, Panagra, did the Western side of Latin America."

fter a short delay, she proceeds, "I had met my future spouse, Doc at San Jose State College, in a French class, and we dated all through school. He was a year behind me and completed his certification while I was an attendant at Pan Am. After with regards to a year we chose to wed, and I needed to leave the aircraft, as those were the guidelines around then. You were unable to be hitched as attendant simultaneously - would you be able to picture that arrangement presently?" asks my mom, and I am immediately helped to remember how various things used to be in the no so distant past.

"What about your life as a USAF spouse? Was it troublesome with every one of the moves at regular intervals?" I ask my mother.

She thinks for a smidgen and afterward answers.

"Doc had been in ROTC in school and not long after we wedded in San Francisco, he was called into the flight preparing in the USAF in

Mission, Texas. We lived in McAllen, Texas for a long time, and afterward continued on to Laredo for six extra months. His first task was Savannah, Ga. At that point, the obligation to the USAF was just a single year. It was a troublesome choice yet after his one year visit, we chose to leave the USAF and we got back to San Francisco where he functioned as a pilot for Pacific Airlines. We both adored residing in the San Francisco region, however Doc, as a lesser aircraft pilot was gone from home constantly. It was then we chose and had the chance to get back to the Air Force and we were positioned in Savannah, Georgia.

When we were positioned there we additionally settled on one more significant choice for our young family, and that choice was to embrace. We applied to a neighborhood halfway house and embraced you when you were just a month and a half old enough!" She shouts with a major wide grin in her face.

I can't resist the urge to snicker and add, "All things considered, I don't recall that as I was close to nothing and have never been famous for my memory abilities!"

She giggles a major snicker at my senseless joke, and I ponder internally that took on or not, a mother will consistently be one's most prominent fan.

Mom happens with her story. "Doc was in the Strategic Air Command or (SAC) and after our task in Savannah, we were appointed to Bermuda and afterward in three years off to Glasgow, Montana. Life in the USAF was hard with a move pretty much like clockwork, yet it was additionally energizing to see new spots and make new companions. It was something we'll generally value and recall.

another conflict had begun in Asia and around 1964-65, Doc was alloted a one year visit in Vietnam while you and I moved to Redding, where Leo and Maria had settled. As you can envision, this was an exceptionally distressing time for our family. Correspondence was restricted to letters and only a couple of calls a day. Yet, we oversaw and Doc returned securely subsequent to serving his country."

"After Vietnam we were appointed to the Apollo program in Patrick AFB, Florida. I was a fourth early age teacher at Indian Harbor Beach Elementary School and Doc flew on the side of a program intended to put a man on the moon. It was an interesting time in our nation and we lived only a couple of miles south of the Cape Canaveral dispatch site. In 1970 we had one more exchange for the family to Andrews AFB close to Washington, DC. Doc flew more modest corporate sort jets called the T-39 on the side of the Pentagon. On our last and last visit with the USAF we moved to Albuquerque where he resigned as a Lt. Col with 20 years of administration to our country. Life was intense moving around so much, however life was great. We met such countless extraordinary families, saw such countless incredible pieces of the US and in general had a great profession in the USAF"

Mom presently says gladly "As a little girl and spouse of pilots in World War II, Vietnam and the Cold War, I can say that it was testing and truly challenging on day to day life, yet in the end we suffered and I accept became more grounded as a family. I realize it made me more grounded and more free personally. As I referenced before, Doc and I never truly felt got comfortable our lives until we resigned and move to Santa Fe, NM where we live today. Would I completely change me? Well no, and parts I had no control of, similar to when my father was an educator during World War II. In any case, being a USAF spouse and every one of the moves were hard for our family however something we just became acquainted with as we made acclimations to new companions, new areas and new schools any place we move. We were family. We were doing a task. We were supporting our country. We adored it and wouldn't transform it. Thinking back in my life, I grew up under the difficulties of the downturn and World War II and being an offspring of a solitary parent. Yet, we made it work and my family is more grounded due to our time at Thunderbird Field."

"Mother that is an extraordinary story," I said. "I never really comprehended the difficulties you and my Grandpa Leo needed to survive. It places things in context when you ponder how fortunate we are today."

"Yet there are difficulties today. Simply unique. Your father and I lived however Cuban Missile emergency, the Kennedy deaths , Vietnam War and the Cold War," she says.

"You flew toward the finish of the Cold War and Gulf Wars". She says. "Various occasions and various difficulties, yet we make due and we push ahead. That is our main event. As a family and as a country."

It's then that I understand that my mother is really an offspring of Thunderbird Field. A survivor, a processor, a warrior.

Man on the Moon

I t was Weaver boys weekend. Me, my 27 year old son, Jonathan (Jo) from Raleigh, NC and my 84 year old dad, RC "Doc" Weaver from Santa Fe, NM. were in town for a National Father and Son Baseball tournament taking place from October 29 to November 2. The tournament was being played on several Major League team spring training facilities around Phoenix. With the help of Airbnb, we were able to rent a "patio" home in the Ahwatukee suburbs, just in the foothills of the beautiful South Mountains. Some folks play golf, our family plays baseball.

As we got comfortable for our first evening, we separated our abilities set to overcome supper. Youthful Weaver-salad. Checked. Great Pa Weaver-burgers. Checked. I oversaw lager, wine and grill. Checked and twofold Checked.

For my 26 year old child, it was somewhat of a home coming. We got the family together and left Vance AFB, Enid, Ok where Jo was brought into the world in 1987. He was an infant when I began F16C preparing close to Luke AFB. Jo, presently a University of Maryland graduate, who concentrated on financial matters, made some available energy from work and was anticipating investing quality time with his father and particularly with his granddad.

It was then Jo asked his granddad an inquiry. "Didn't distant grandpa Leo flight educate around here?"

Captain RC "Doc" Weaver flying the KC 135

Doc replied by saying, "Not far off at Thunderbird Field. Allow me to recount to you a little story.

nd let me explain why I see myself as an inheritance pilot of Thunderbird Field."

What does that mean precisely?" asked Jo as he opened the principal jug of brew of the evening.

My dad in-law, your incredible granddad Leo Purinton, was a teacher at Thunderbird Field, simply over those mountains" as we as a whole looked at an excellent Arizona nightfall. "It was in Glendale only 10 miles from where we're remaining at present.

But let me back up and recount to you my story and what the set of experiences and custom of the popular landing strip meant for my life and those of my family for a long time into the future" said Doc as he took a taste of wine.

It was the conclusion of the downturn age in the United States when I was brought into the world in Milwaukee, Wisconsin on May 5, 1932. I had an early appreciation for flying. As I think back now, I can see that a profession in flying was a characteristic for me." He said.

"My first real openness to flying was after World War II when I was a youthful young person. Weave Reeves, the originator of Reeves

Alaskan Airlines, flew into Madison, Wisconsin, to visit my dad. The obscurity of time and a bustling life leaves me dumbfounded with respect to why this significant man flew in to see my dad. Yet, whatever the explanation, I am ever appreciative that he did." He proceeds, "Mr Reeves arrived at Truxx Field one day in an open cockpit airplane. I, alongside my dad and the whole Weaver family, was at the air terminal to welcome Mr. Reeves. I'll always remember the second when I saw Mr. Reeves land that staggering airplane. It was the most intriguing thing I'd at any point found in all my years. That second left very effect – indeed, it had an enduring impression one that suffered for the remainder of my life. My affection for avionics was conceived that day and has never disappeared.

Mr. Reeves was a savvy and attentive man. He could see the sheer wonderment all over. After he examined with my dad whatever business they had met to lead, he turned and checked out me. My heart was in my throat when he inclined down and inquired as to whether I would be keen on a trip around the air terminal. I thought I had kicked the bucket and gone to paradise – and my folks knew it. They partook in the rush I was encountering when Mr. Reeves helped me into the passenger seat of the two-seater after which he crept in the back in the pilot's seat. Obviously I was smiling from one ear to another – nothing might have removed that grin. I was cheerful and regarded to be imparting the cockpit to an eminent flight legend like Bob Reeves."

"That must be cool" Jo added.

Definitely it was, Jo!" Grandpa Doc said and proceeded, "The memory of that first flight never lost its wizardry however it was a drawn-out period of time before I had the option to truly seek after a profession in avionics. In 1947 my family moved to Los Angeles where my sibling Cliff and I went to Harvard School, a tactical institute in the San Fernando Valley. After graduation, I went to San Jose State University and enlisted in the Air Force ROTC and was a part from 1950 through 1954. While in school, I had the option to set aside a tad of cash and took a few flying illustrations at a neighborhood air terminal close to San Jose, California. I held back on all the other things – including suppers and celebrating – so I could set to the side the cash for flying illustrations.

Captain Doc Weaver wearing Thunderbird cowhide protective cap given to him by Leo Purinton

As it turned out my adoration for flying came to play a more significant part in my life than I at any point expected and demonstrated not to be a fleeting curiosity. I had studied expressive arts and was viewed as a promising craftsman, yet I was down to earth and perceived that I would have to get by for me and possibly for a family and that being a destitute craftsman would likely not give the income I would require for a respectable way of life. It was around that time that I elected to enter the United States Air Force pilot preparing program. I was restless to begin however like all the other things throughout everyday life, things won't ever occur when you need them to. My hang tight for pilot preparing school after graduation would be an extremely long a half year."

"What did you do meanwhile?" asked Jo.

"I utilized my time." Answered Doc. "While hanging tight the a half year for pilot preparing to start, Alyce Purinton, my school darling and I chose to steal away to San Francisco where we were hitched on December 1, 1954. Obviously, while we were dating I regularly heard tales about her dad, Leo Purinton, who was incredible in those parts. He started flying during the 1920s and later proceeded to turn into a PT-17 (Stearman) Instructor pilot during World War II at the famous Thunderbird Field in Glendale, Arizona.

Leo and his family resided in Yreka, California and at the main chance I needed to move away from school, Alyce and I drove up to Yreka where I met Leo and starting there on everything we did was discussion about flying. He might have been my dad in-law, yet we were siblings in soul. The Second Great War had as of late finished and there appeared to be a constant flow of youngsters who became keen on the workmanship and art of flying.

Perhaps they'd been motivated by the refined and valorous pilots who had assisted the Allies with accomplishing triumph. Any young fellow or lady who lived in Northern California or close by who needed to figure out how to fly, Leo was the man to see. His standing as an astounding pilot and patient and able teacher spread all over. He was a Fixed Base Operator and had flying activities at two air terminals right outside of Yreka. One was the Montague Airport and the different was Siskiyou County Airport. Since I had a month left before I entered USAF pilot preparing, I chose to exploit the personal time. Alyce and I climbed to Yreka so Leo could begin helping me to fly. It was perhaps the best choice I at any point made."

"Similar story for me too as I worked with Leo before going off to pilot training. Who needs something to drink?" I added.

Lt. RC Weaver T33 "Hero" shot. UPT. Circa 1951

"Upon graduation from primary pilot training, Alyce and I drove up the Rio Grande to Laredo, Texas, for my six-month basic program in the Lockheed T-33.

I immediately could sense that I had a leg up on the other trainees because of my good fortune in having Leo as my instructor in aviation fundamentals. As graduation approached my flight instructors at Laredo wanted me to stay on as an instructor – apparently some of Leo's teaching magic had rubbed off on me!" Doc said as he laughed a little.

"At that time I really didn't have a clue whether or not a career in the Air Force was for me. Since I was uncertain about where my future would take me and the commitment was three years after graduation, I turned down   the

assignment. I opted instead to accept a tour at Hunter AFB, Georgia, to fly the KC-97 in the Strategic Air Command (SAC). It was another decision that I never regretted.

At the end of the three-year tour in Savannah, Alyce and I elected to leave the USAF and move back closer to California to be near family. But no matter where I was geographically, my passion for aviation never wavered. After a year, I was hired to fly DC-3s with Pacific Airlines and was based out our favorite city, San Francisco. All my hours of training and service in the Air Force had been rewarded."

"Hard work pays off" I added, as my father quietly nods while looking at Jo, trying to measure how much of all this is registering with him.

fter sipping some of his wine, Doc continues with his story. "Although we celebrated initially, after one year with Pacific Airlines, we decided the airline lifestyle was not suited for us – there were too many long hours and days of separation and with the pressure of the huge responsibility that was inherent in piloting a large commercial aircraft, we decided that I should resign and re-enter the USAF. The Air Force had felt like home to us and it was where we belonged.

Throughout the late 1950s and early 1960s I was reassigned back to my old unit at Hunter AFB, Savannah, Georgia, for a year and then reassigned to Bermuda. President John F. Kennedy was in the White House battling the Cuban Missile Crisis and the US was fighting the Cold War with the USSR. Our unit's primary mission was to refuel strategic bombers flying between the United States and North Africa. After the Cuban Missile Crisis ended and the world could take a deep breath, I upgraded to the USAF's newest refueling tanker, the KC-135 and moved the family to Glasgow AFB, Montana. We felt Big Sky country would be a great place to raise our kids.

In 1964 the Vietnam War was well under way and I volunteered for a worldwide reassignment to fly the C123 Provider with the 309th Air Commando Squadron to and from the battle zone. Our primary mission was to fly supplies and troops throughout Southern Vietnam and on special missions we were qualified to spray Agent Orange thought at the time to be an effective way to make the enemy more visible and thus more vulnerable. Agent Orange or Herbicide Orange (HO) was a herbicide and defoliant that was sprayed on the enemy's supply routes and food supplies throughout Vietnam, eastern Laos and parts of Cambodia. In short order Agent Orange killed off the heavy foliage that shielded the movements of the enemy. It made the supply chain an easy target for aerial attack. Of course initially, the US government had no idea of the impact that Agent Orange would have upon the health of innocent locals and our own soldiers."

o now is listening very closely, perhaps the stories about Vietnam are more engaging to him as it's relatively nearer in time and still a fresh wound in our collective memory.

"I didn't know your health was at risk, grandpa!" Jo exclaimed. "That had to be terrifying too for grandma Alyce!"

Doc nods and goes on to say: "The program was called Operation Ranch Hand and the mission was met with minor success but after the war the numerous health issues for both troops and civilians on the ground began to be surface. For years, the prospect of contracting illnesses caused by Agent Orange loomed over us. Like many veterans, every year we were flown to Houston or other medical centers around the country for a full medical evaluation to discover if we suffered any side effects from our contact with Agent Orange. Statistics indicated that the chemical increased normal rates of cancer, nerve damage, skin disorders as well as higher than normal rates of leukemia and Hodgkin's lymphoma. I was one of the lucky ones with no major health issues ever manifesting. But it was a constant worry for the twenty years of regular examinations and the continuing medical research that was conducted. Vietnam was a very demanding assignment but like most who served in combat, we were proud of the work we accomplished in defense of our country and in support of our nation's troops.

Captain Weaver working the Apollo 11 command post.
Man landed on the moon July 19, 1969

After my Vietnam tour, we moved the family to my next assignment at Patrick AFB, Florida, where I flew in support of the National Aeronautics and Space Administration (NASA) and the Apollo program. The Apollo program was part of President John F. Kennedy's national goal of landing a man on the moon and returning him safely to Earth by the end of the decade. It was an ambitious government project which involved billions of dollars, employed over 400,000 people and was supported by over 20,000 companies and universities." He continues.

"During my NASA assignment, I flew a modified KC-135 that had a "snoopy nose" on the front-end of the aircraft. The KC-135 was designed to carry specialized communications system to help monitor the launch and recovery of the astronauts. Several of our support missions included flying
00 nm (nautical miles) in "race track" patterns over the Pacific Ocean between New Zealand and Hawaii.

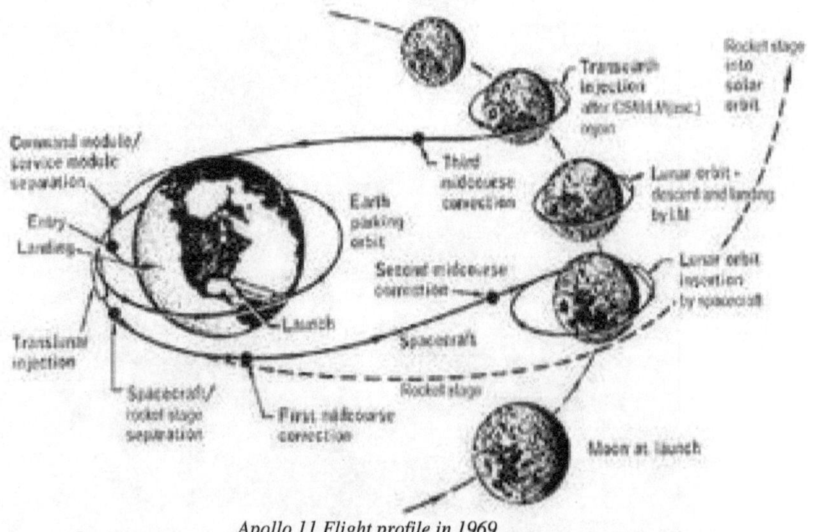

Apollo 11 Flight profile in 1969

And when we were not flying missions on the other side of the world, we were attached to the Command Center to provide support between the USAF and NASA."

"It was an exciting time. NASA and the astronauts were making history and our unit was part of it. As every schoolchild knows, on July 19-21, 1969, Apollo 11 landed on the moon and Buzz Aldrin and Neil Armstrong walked on the moon and returned safely to Earth. Kennedy's national goal was met and it was a very proud time to not only be a member of the armed services, but, more importantly, to be part of a successful team that helped to put the first humans on the moon. But not every school kid knows that your dad was born on July 19, 1959, and he spent his 10th birthday believing the celebrations were in his honor !!!"

Lt. Col "Doc" Weaver's USAF patches

Both Jo and myself let out a good laugh at my father making fun of me. "After a tour at Andrews AFB, just outside of Washington DC and

Kirtland AFB in Albuquerque, NM, it was time to retire but my love of aviation did not falter. I was fortunate enough to retire after 20+ years of service and an exciting and rewarding career doing something that I loved. I was able to satisfy my love for aviation while serving my country. Alyce and I moved to Santa Fe, NM where we live today some forty years later. Looking back on it all now from the start of my flying career, I recognize how important my first few hours of instruction time with Leo Purinton was in helping me to enjoy a successful and challenging career in aviation. I was honored to be part of the legacy pilots of Thunderbird Field. I was filled with

a pride that is difficult to describe when your dad, joined the ranks of flyers as the third generation of pilots in our family." Doc finishes.

"Wow, grandpa, those are some adventures you've have in life. I never knew that flying had done some much for you !" Said Jo, genuinely impressed at his grandpa life story being told all at once.

"Being a pilot, would do that for you….Obviously, the love of aviation is in our family DNA." I say.

Now who wants more burgers?!"

Hometown Hero

It's O'dark-thirty Monday morning and I'm heading to the Reagan National Airport (DCA) to catch the first flight of the day to work out of Miami (MIA). Like most of my commutes, I'm on the jump seat of the Boeing 737. But it's a seat on an airplane going to work, a personal choice and all part of being a commuter pilot.

ommuters, like myself, enjoy the international flying because of the "quality of life" issues. Most international or wide body flying, typically are more efficient, meaning they pay more and there is less time away from base or home. Also, most are all nighters, meaning, just as it sounds, the flight occurs at night on both legs, going and forth. But with three pilots it's not too bad. On the plus side, it's easier to commute to and from work because you have most of the day to get there and back. I know, the glamorous life and the things a commercial pilot has to deal with!

oday, I am flying a domestic trip for a change. Flight AA 101, Miami to Los Angeles. It's a 2-day trip to help fill my monthly schedule. It's only worth 12 hours of flight time, but it's a nice layover in LA and only a 30 minute bike ride to Manhattan Beach and a "spit in the ocean"; a term of endearment. Fish tacos and beers in the afternoon when we get in and an early bike ride to a workout, coffee on the beach in the morning when we leave.

After a successful flight over and uneventful 24 hours layover, the next day, the crew and I head back to the LAX terminal to meet our jet at gate 42. I give a friendly "hello" to the gate agent and ask her if she would mind letting us down the jet bridge, so as to complete our pre-flight duties for our return trip to Miami. Out of the corner of my eye walks up a familiar face.   It

takes me about two seconds to realize it's an old friend that I haven't seen in over two decades. It's Steve Rickert!

Steve recently checked out as a Captain on the Airbus 319/320. He himself
is a commuter from Redding, California to Miami and today he has a jump seat in the cockpit of our 777 heading east bound. No problem, it gives us 4 hours to catch up and reminisce about our first instructor pilot Leo Purinton.

"Hey Steve...great to see you again!" I greet him.

"You too, Scott...looks like the flight is full, you guys mind giving me a ride to work?" replies Steve as we shake hands.

"No problem for a fellow commuter. Come on down, and put your bags up, we have a lot to get caught up on." I say.

I've been meaning to call you and ask for some help in a little project of mine." I add.

Lt. Col.'s Scott Weaver and Steve Rickert, AA 777 from LAX to MIA

"What's that? I can't wait to hear more!" says Steve.

I am researching material for a book about Leo and his flying career at Thunderbird Field. It's about aviation history from WWII to the Cold War." I explain.

"Wow, that's very cool!" says Steve.

"Also, part of the book will be about legacy pilots who were trained by Leo. You, me and even my dad and his career in the USAF. Vietnam and NASA. I think your story would fit just nicely in there ! Would you mind sharing it with me, Steve?" I explain to Steve, as I finish up my pre-flight cockpit duties for our flight to Miami.

Steve looks genuinely interested. "Oh wow, what a great idea! I never thought of myself as a legacy pilot of anyone let alone one from Thunderbird Field. I'd love to, always happy to remember the good ole days!"

"Tell me how you got started flying?" When we first met you were flying canceled checks around in a twin and I was just a ramp rat at Redding Airport" I said.

Steve starts telling me all about his story and I'm happy to have this opportunity to reconnect with him and add to the story "I first met Leo when I was a college student at Shasta College, a two-year community college in Redding, California. Although having enough college credits to move onto a four-year school wasn't a problem, I had just begun my third year at the college. I felt aimless; my life had no direction and there was absolutely nothing that interested me and I was sure that nothing ever would. I couldn't imagine a career in business or in a technical industry. I had pursued various subjects in school but nothing inspired me or had a lasting impact on me.

As I mentioned, I had plenty of college credits but I had reached no comfort level when thinking long-term career wise. I attributed it to being immature, unfocused and undisciplined. But it was worrisome. I had to do something worthwhile with my life – my parents were both successful business owners. I remained at the community college rather than apply to a four-year college because of this lack of direction. During my first two years at Shasta, I was enrolled in pre-med classes. Although I had passing grades, my performance was mediocre and deep down I knew that I wasn't cut out for a career as a physician. It just sounded good especially to my parents." He continued.

In my third year at Shasta I kind of started all over and enrolled in a

different mix of classes so that I could explore other opportunities and possibilities. Leo Purinton was an instructor in one of those classes, an aviation ground school program. A requirement of the class was ultimately qualifying for a private pilot's license.

I was already somewhat acquainted with Leo. My father and mother had met Leo through their family business and I knew he was a pilot. I had done some part time work for my parents at their business concern but had never formally met Leo prior to my enrolment in his class. I recalled that my dad had once taken me when I was just thirteen to Leo's airport, Redding Sky Ranch, where I was introduced to Leo's son Mike and took a short flight with him that afternoon; however, Leo was not present during this visit.

My father knew I had very little interest in anything. Looking back I recognized that this visit was his attempt to inspire me about flying. But like everything else during my teen years, I was not impressed and the memory of the flight and any excitement I may have felt at the time soon faded. I never gave the incident much thought and it failed to instil within me any desire to be a part of the aviation industry."

"Hold on Steve, let me finish the taxi checklist. You know how busy LAX gets around this time in the morning." I say to Steve as I get on going with the last details before take-off.

teve is really into his story now and he carries on with it… "I do remember talking to Leo shortly after I began my college aviation ground school class. I asked to speak with him following my first two classes. He was very open and eager to answer all my questions. He filled me in on his background and experiences and that he currently taught flight lessons at Redding Municipal Airport. It was his love of aviation that made him an excellent teacher. His enthusiasm for flying impressed his students, even those who like me didn't know where they belonged and hadn't found their niche in life. His love for flying slowly but surely began to rub off on me."

manage to get a few sentences in between Steve's story as he takes a sip of water. "Leo never gave me the "love of flying" briefing. I think he assumed since my dad was a pilot in the USAF that I would be talking with him about flying as a career. I never felt like there was a "calling" for me or that flying was in my DNA. Flying was simple in some regards, but the real challenge was the combination hand eye coordination and the discipline Leo expected when flying."

I understand," replies Steve. "It wasn't long before he convinced me to

begin actual flight lessons with him. I didn't realize it at the time, but flying was fairly easy for me as I had always enjoyed any type of motorized vehicle or craft. Being a great teacher who had an innate intuition about his students, he may have recognized that I was a good prospect for becoming a pilot. Cars, boats, motorcycles and tractors were always fascinating to me. I think that airplanes and flying was just part of the organic attraction I had for motorized land and sea craft.

After about eight lessons with Leo, he one day surprised me and asked me to stop the aircraft before take-off but not shut down the engine. He crawled out on the wing of that Piper Warrior II after we stopped and told me it was time for me to go solo. Much to my surprise and I must admit my initial horror, he told me that I didn't need him anymore. I was on my own – he was my lifeline, my crutch and I was going to have to do without him! It didn't do any good to protest. Once he made a decision about a flight student's level of ability, there was no debating it. He didn't give me time to respond to his proclamation – he headed off quickly to the office to wait for my return. Reflecting back I remember many things flashing through my mind. Would I make it back?! And if so, would I make it back in one piece?! A trainee's first solo flight required three touch and goes and a final landing to a full stop. I was instructed to stay in the local pattern and to complete the day by myself.

But Leo knew what he was doing. He knew I was ready – he never would have placed any of his students in jeopardy. He had a good read on his students and knew who was ready to go solo and who needed more training hours. My first solo flight went well, and I was very happy once I returned and was given big congratulations from Leo and from the office staff. Not long after returning, I was surprised to see Leo approaching me with a pair of scissors. He instructed me to turn around. To my astonishment he proceeded to cut out a large piece out of the back of my shirt. He marked that piece of my shirt with the date and aircraft number as well as his signature."

"This is all great stuff !!!" I say.

As the 777-200 rolls down the 27R and starts its initial climb to 10,000' with a large left hand turn over the Pacific Ocean, Steve continues with his story.

"This ritual to memorialize a pilot's first solo has long been a tradition in aviation, as you know. The cut and signed shirt tail was normally placed on the wall of the local Fixed Base Operation of the local airport. I feel certain that that piece of my aviation history still exists somewhere and   I'm

determined to someday find it. It meant a lot to me and marked a turning point in my life and career goals."

This memory hits home, and I start recalling what my first solo was like "It's been a few years, but I remember that for me, it was after a long hot day working on the ramp. Leo had me do a quick flight to do some area work, Lazy 8's, chandelles and some stalls. It was starting to get late, and the sun was starting to set and he asked me to head back to the pattern at Redding Municipal. There was no one in the traffic pattern for runway 34. The air was calm and the landings were coming easy that day. Without warning he asks me to taxi off at the cross runway 12/30 where he then gets out of the plane and says… "you got it, now go give me 3 touch and goes before the sun set and we have to make this a night flight.

You never forget your first solo. You awareness level goes up. Your situation awareness seems keener. There is a sense of pride, knowing your instructor has enough confidence to cut your loose with such a large responsibility.

When I returned and parked the plane, Leo was there with a pair scissors and the "cutting of Tee shirt" tradition. I was wearing my favorite "PIPER" shirt and hated getting it cut, but in the end it was well worth giving it up for my solo flight."

teve smiles and nods his head as he continues with his story: "That solo flight for me was in December of 1977, and by May of 1978 I had finally received my private pilot license. To some, that might seem like quite a while but most pilots acquire about 45-55 hours of flight time before taking their official flight check that enables them to receive their certificates. Well that wasn't the case with my training or what Leo had in mind for me. After about another ten hours of flight after my maiden solo, Leo encouraged me to fly another type of aircraft different than the Piper Cherokee that I had all of training on. He suggested that I fly the Bellanca Decathlon, a tail dragger (tail wheel steering) aircraft that had aerobatic capabilities. He must have seen something in me at the time that I failed to see in myself. I was encouraged by his confidence in me. I knew I had to work at attaining that same level of confidence in myself."

"Without a doubt, Leo probably seen some military pilot potential in you at an early piece of your preparation." I say to Steve, and I know it in all sincerity, as my grandpa was not a simple educator.

Steve laughs and proceeds. "Leo had me fixed for the adrenaline junkie I

never realized I was. In any case, his instinctive sense was perfect. When I got into aerobatics, I was sold. Indeed, even in my first airborne trip to become familiar with this new expertise, we started with circles, rolls and twists, and snap rolls. It was surely a rush for me as I was an amusement park ride addict growing up, and this was what absolutely set the snare for me in flying. At last, I truly needed to turn into a piece of something. A couple of flights later, I was flying the aerobatic Decathlon solo just as the Cherokee and ready to do gymnastics all alone. As it turned out I was a characteristic and Leo, in the entirety of his insight, had known it.

I review Leo discussing me and aerobatics with a portion of his pals on the ground after flight and chuckling about me not having the option to see out the front window when we were upset in flight. The normal individual would not be giggling at such a new development. However, pilots, particularly aerobatics pilots, addressed what was still wild and free in America – we resembled the ranchers of the sky. The airplane had couple seating, with the teacher sitting in the back seat. When transformed my hair which was very long – after all it was 70s and I was a free thinker – clouded my front facing vision. I was very astounded whenever this first occurred and couldn't see past my hair. Luckily I made due and joyfully recounted my experience for quite a long time a while later. Leo had a team trimmed at that point and evidently was very interested at this young fellow whose hair was long to the point that it clouded his vision while topsy turvy and sideways as we sped through the skies at a decent clasp.

While finishing the preparation towards my private permit, Leo was approached to get a pristine Piper Warrior II from the plant at Vero Beach, Florida. Since I had not done any crosscountry preparing yet, a ten-hour prerequisite for the private permit, Leo inquired as to whether I needed to come so I could get additional hours during the full circle from Northern California to Florida and return. It was an awesome open door for myself and an opportunity to meet a portion of Leo's flight family, his child and little girl, Mike and Marilyn, who lived in Dallas, TX and Alyce and Doc, your folks, who lived in Santa Fe, NM. His family had a significant avionics foundation, as you probably are aware Scott, with Mike and Marilyn flying for the aircrafts and Doc being a resigned Air Force pilot. I trust Alyce, your mother may have been an airline steward also, yet not entirely certain with regards to that, the memory blurs a digit here. This was additionally my first chance to truly fly and see the US something I had never experienced."

"Interesting that you recall that, my mother has some airline steward experience added to her repertoire ! An incredible memory you have, Steve !"

"Most new pilots possibly get to encounter short crosscountry preparing flights when leading their preparation. I perceived that I was lucky to be allowed this opportunity, an encounter that was particularly valued toward the start of my profession." Steve proceeds. "Subsequent to finishing my private permit, Leo kept on coaching me and give direction at whatever point I hit an obstruction. He alongside his child Mike gave me the support I expected to keep seeking after an aeronautics profession. Their unfaltering help and trust in me eventually persuaded me that I could have a profession in avionics and have the option to do what I wanted to do and be essential for an industry that was energizing and testing. I before long felt that I could achieve this with their assistance and made arrangements to proceed with the pathway to turn into an expert pilot, a pathway that had surprisingly showed up before me.

Leo was consistently the quintessential expert and was devoted to the norms and guidelines that controlled the aeronautics business, yet there were some close to home episodes including Leo that consistently make me grin when I review them. My mom shared a portion of these accounts as of late. My dad had for a long time needed to fly yet never truly had an exceptionally sure outlook on his capacity to turn into a capable pilot. Unexpectedly since he was a horrible vehicle driver he figured he'd be surprisingly more dreadful attempting to fly noticeable all around. He was sure he wouldn't make a decent pilot. Knowing my dad, I think he definitely needed to have the option to travel and investigate the world from the air.

Naturally he generally needed to chat with Leo when Leo went to my people's meat market. Be that as it may, Leo had somewhat of a standing for being economical which some might arrange as "modest". Our meat was really evaluated above most different business sectors because of the nature of the meat and our predominant maturing process. Our costs mirrored our top notch norms. Notwithstanding, Leo consistently needed a decent arrangement and spread the word about that when shopping at our market. Relatives alternated with representatives in the market so that there wasn't a similar individual continually working the counter.

However with Leo's tenacious method of pushing at a superior cost, my mom – who was an extremely understanding individual – at last had it with him and would not look out for him. She truly had come to disdain Leo. I'm certain she was fairly shocked that I had appreciated his conversation whenever I had started flying with him. She didn't recount to me a portion of the anecdotes about Leo until some other time in my profession. She presumably didn't have any desire to do or say whatever would affect the excitement I had for flight since I at long last observed what I needed to do throughout everyday life.

As time continued and I went flying with my folks, the perceived the amount I delighted in flying and that Leo's motivation had been focal in spurring me to settle on a profession in aeronautics. They were entirely thankful, to the point that their rebellious child had a top dog that a dear fellowship started to develop among Leo and my folks, particularly my mom. My mom who had at first not been a fan had the option to look past Leo's forceful way and like the positive job he had played in her child's life."

am somewhat shocked by this remark, yet certain enough, I perceive my granddad in there… I disclose to Steve, "Leo was tight with his cash. Be that as it may, take a gander at where he came from. Take a gander at where his age came from. The downturn time. Each time I eat an apple I'm helped to remember Leo."

"Why would that be?" Steve inquires.

"Leo would eat the whole apple, center and all." I answer. "He would let me know that as a child he and his siblings would go days without full dinners and that missing piece of the apple was food he wasn't willing to miss. Right up 'til the present time, I never take a gander at an apple without thinking about that story that my granddad imparted to me."

The plane scopes cruising elevation of FL350 as the story proceeds.

Steve sits peacefully for a couple of moments, contemplating that, prior to proceeding with his story. "Eventually Leo and Mom talked on the telephone frequently about my flying, a dear fellowship additionally created among her and Marie, Leo's better half. My mom actually has a plant given to her by Marie that she named "Marie" and has taken various cuttings from the plant to provide for other people. Right up 'til today that plant is in her receiving area, sound as could be. It's a demonstration of the past and to her adoration and reverence for two old buddies.

Leo had a skill for bringing you into his reality and making you a player in his family. His child Mike and girl Marilyn were warm and liberal when I was starting my vocation and leading flight preparing in the Dallas region. They permitted me to remain with them for a very long time before I happened to school. Mike was useful in kicking me off at the flying school he went to in Oklahoma and furthermore permitted me sit in a few B727 test systems while he was leading guidance meetings for Braniff Airlines. His whole family couldn't have been more useful when I truly required it – toward the beginning of my youngster profession in flying."

That truly illustrates what was going on with the family" I say for all to hear.

Steve continues and tells me, "With the assistance of Mike Purinton, I applied and

was acknowledged at the very school that he joined in, Southeastern Oklahoma State University. I finished school in July 1979, and started searching for that first genuine aeronautics work. I didn't have a lot of involvement and lamentably around then, the US economy was easing back and numerous carrier pilots had been furloughed. I had found my fantasy calling however the interest for my abilities and capacities had abruptly plunged. This, obviously, made for an exceptionally helpless beginning for my vocation. In any case, I endured. I had observed my vocation and I wasn't going to allow a wavering economy to debilitate me. I was lucky to find some work as a flight teacher in Reno, NV in late 1979.

just stood firm on the educator's footing a brief time frame. I was offered and acknowledged a position flying mail on the evening plan among Reno and Las Vegas. After with regards to a year and half later I had the option to get a comparative line of work at Redding Municipal Airport and moved back to where I had grown up. In the mid year of 1982, I was acquainted with Leo's grandson, it was you, obviously, Scott, and you had come to Redding to visit and figure out how to fly. Before long you procured your private pilot's permit – you were another regular pilot very much like your granddad. You would have rather not persevere through the extensive regular citizen preparing course that I had gone through and before long figuring out how to fly, you chose to enlist in the US Air Force to turn into a pilot. I kept in touch with you while you continued through preparing. Also, you kept on asking me to enlist in the Air Force, yet I truly didn't have the interest to join. Recollect ? The tactical life wasn't so much for me."

That's right, I recall all that." I say.

"As I referenced prior, the economy was in a descending twisting during this time. The aircrafts weren't recruiting and many organizations were failing. I was flying regular contracts for legal counselors to the Sacramento Courts for judicial actions. I was not raking in huge profits on these sanctions and was left sitting at air terminals for a really long time, for quite a while. I had a lot of free time and combined with my low income I started to believe that maybe I should seek after another, more rewarding and solid method for making money. It was during one of my personal times when I was in a holding up design at the Sacramento air terminal that I considered you, Scott, and your asking to enlist in the Air Force. The possibility of surrendering aeronautics as a vocation constrained me to settle on a decision that would genuinely completely change me. I reached a similar Air Force spotter that you had gone through to join the military. This was most likely the best choice I might have at any point made as a youthful pilot."

I can't really accept that we wound up utilizing a similar enrollment specialist and afterward had nearly

equal vocations from that point !" I shout .

Steve proceeds to let me know a tad about his time in the USAF. "In 1983 I started my profession in United States Air Force. Official preparing school was three months since quite a while ago followed quickly by pilot preparing where we flew two airplanes, the T-37 and afterward advanced onto the T-38, a supersonic airplanes that is as yet being used today. I surely had an edge on most pilots entering flight school with almost 4,000 flight hours added to my repertoire prior to entering Air Force preparing. Likely the greatest assistance I had in my accomplishment in the Air Force is the thing that I took in as a youngster from Leo. The spot arrival preparing under Leo as a youthful understudy just as the high level aerobatic and tail wheel experience was an important upgrade to my Air Force preparing. That preparation assisted me with dominating and finish at the highest point of my group. Subsequent to preparing I was offered my best option of airplane, the F-15 Eagle."

"I wasn't quite as great or fortunate as you. Completing at the highest point of your group was a significant privilege, yet Leo saw your latent capacity. For my purposes, I tell individuals it took me four years to get past UPT… one year as an understudy and three as a T38 teacher pilot (IP) !" I joke and snicker at my own joke.

Flying the F15C, Captain Steve Rickert and previous Thunderbird Instructor Leo Purinton at the

Steve laughs. He happens with his story: "Subsequent to flying the F-15 for a year or thereabouts, I got some information about the chance of some time or another getting back to my old neighborhood with that stream. For the following four years I was informed that it wouldn't be imaginable. However at that point in 1990, I was adequately fortunate to get back to Redding where I had figured out how to initially fly, with a McDonnell Douglas F-15A Eagle.

eturning to Redding in the smooth Eagle stream was a pleased day made more uncommon by being welcomed by Leo with great affection and a major "congrats." I realize he was however glad as I seemed to be to be remaining there together that day. I let Leo in on that everything began with him."

"That is extraordinary stuff, Steve !" I shout as we start our VNAV drop runway 12 into Miami. "I can't completely accept that how quick the flight went Steve. Finish your story."

"There is a photograph of Leo and me settling on the landing area. It was remembered for an article about Air Show '90. The article gave some foundation data on Leo and me. It referenced that I had worked at North Star Aviation – which was the sanction organization – and that my fretfulness concerning that position prompted my enlisting in the Air Force. The correspondent got that right! The article proceeded to say that I was a stream pilot educator. It cited me as saying that my understudies had "as of now been to direct school so I don't train them to fly. I'm showing them how to battle and get by in a dogfight.

When reviewing the entirety of the insight and mentorship that Leo gave me, I think about his certifiable love for avionics and active flying. He had extraordinary stick and rudder abilities, incredible air sense and an undying craving to coach the people who he felt would share that equivalent enthusiasm for flying. He generally had an inspirational perspective on life and that extended to his energy, fellowships, family and flying. Due to Leo, I have partaken in a brilliant profession in flight." As Steve completes his story, we have a common smooth landed in Miami and a short taxi to door D27.

I shake Steve's hand, let him know how extraordinary it was finding out the latest and in particular say thanks to him for sharing his account of how his flying vocation began and particularly his anecdotes about his first flight educator Leo Purinton.

ot surprisingly, I race to my suburbanite trip back to Washington, wishing I had more opportunity to visit with Steve.

"Lt. Col. Rickert is a genuine inheritance pilot of Leo Purinton and Thunderbird

Field," is the last idea that enters my thoughts as I shut my eyes and make myself agreeable in my seat by the window that will take me home.

Baseball and Apple Pie

As a kid growing up I never had a strong desire to become a pilot. I'd been around airplanes all my life but had no urge to start flying at an early age.

My dad had a long term vocation in the USAF. My uncle soloed at 15 years of age. also, was flying business with Brannif Airlines. Obviously, my granddad was in the flying industry his whole life. I went through hours around his fix based activity (FBO), tidying up cigarette butts, espresso cups and soft drink bottle covers. Whenever given a possibility I was continually snatching rides in the secondary lounge of planes with my granddad and his understudy. In any case, that was their obsession not mine.

y enthusiasm was baseball. In the same way as other children, I longed for only baseball. I adored playing different games growing up. Wrestling, soccer, football
- they all were source for me to contend and a method for meeting new companions since my father moved like clockwork with his USAF profession. However, baseball was my genuine affection and I thought I'd have a chance to play proficient. At Valley High School in Albuquerque, New Mexico, I was explored by Cincinnati Reds and the Los Angeles Dodgers. I was selected by numerous individuals of the universities in the Southwest district to incorporate New Mexico, Arizona and Colorado. At a certain point, my father even proposed the US Air Force Academy, yet I was past the point of no return in their extended application process. After some school visits in Colorado, nearly as a bit of hindsight, I made a speedy visit to the Air Force Academy in Colorado Springs. Yet, in the wake of watching cadets walk in 90 degree points around the grounds, eating "complete dinners" during lunch and seeing not many young ladies, there was

minimal possibility I was going to the foundation.

    t snowed the night prior to my selecting visit to University of Colorado. A bright spring day with a new cover of snow nearby and Flat Irons at

the foundation of the Colorado Rockies, it was delightful. So when Coach Irv Brown called and offered a grant to play baseball in Boulder, Colorado, I took it. However, much to My dismay what difficulties laid ahead me.

    he main test of school baseball was the early morning exercises. I despised starting off right on time! Second test of school baseball, particularly in Colorado, was the cool, wet and blanketed spring climate. We may just get outside a few times before our season started in mid February. Then, I was enrolled as a pitcher just when I was really a very decent center infielder. In High School I played each pitch. Be that as it may, pitchers in school don't play each game and when you're not tossing a warm up area meeting, you're running. Furthermore, when you're not running, you're hitting a fungo (more modest bat) for infield. I got truly adept at hitting fungos. Ultimately, Colorado had to drop it's long term baseball program from its varsity status because of a government administering called Title IX. It was a law fundamentally ordering that assuming government financing was going to state funded colleges, then, at that point, they were needed to even out all kinds of people athletic groups.

    With just two years to go and no baseball to play, I chose to concentrate on finishing my certificate. In 1981, I graduated with a Bachelor of Science in Business with a minor in software engineering. At a youthful age, I could see the fate of PCs not too far off and thought I would be advised to be ready to look for a job in the new profession field of PC innovation. Much to My dismay at that point, yet I wound up residing just a pretty far from Steve Jobs and Steve Wozniak carport where they began Apple PCs.

    ***

efore tracking down work with IBM in San Jose and the destined to be renamed "Silicon Valley", I was voyaging and working my direction around the United States. West coast to east drift, and on my subsequent trip west bound, I took off to Northern California to procure my pilot's permit anticipating me at the now renowned Thunderbird Pilots house - Leo Purinton.

I had my first flight example with Leo. My granddad's standing as an intense flight teacher went before him. He was scaring. At just 5' 10", yet a thick 200 lbs, with wide shoulders and a 60's style level top hair style.

What I recollect him first showing me was the significance of a decent handshake. He had huge amazing hands. I could simply envision the strength that came from many years of difficult work on vehicles, box plants and later as an airplane technician. "Keep it firm and keep it solid" he generally said. He'd try to shake my hand before each flight illustration, as though we had recently met for

the initial time.

My granddad was in his mid 70's the point at which I began preparing with him. He'd been flying beginning around 1927 and began educating about 10 years after the fact. Over 55+ long periods of involvement and 10,000 hours of flight time, the majority of it as an educator. After WWII and Thunderbird Field he had freedoms to remain in the US Army Air Corp or fly business with Pan Am or TWA, yet he needed to educate. That was his affection, his energy. He moved to Oregon for a couple of years, then, at that point, gotten comfortable Northern California where he purchased his own private landing strip called Redding Sky Ranch which was only south of town. He never had a lot of cash or needed excessively, yet he generally advised me to accomplish something you really cherish and be great at it.

It was 1982 when Leo began preparing me. He had as of late sold that air terminal south of Redding yet kept up with his guaranteed flight teacher (CFI) appraisals and was just preparing a couple "exceptional" understudies at that point. I was one of his understudies yet with no exceptional advantages. Being his grandson implied no uncommon treatment, no sir! I was dealt with solidly and was relied upon to try sincerely and be ready for each flight.

I was employed as a lineman or "mechanic" chipping away at the incline and around the holder region. I got and conveyed airplane parts. I washed, cleaned and waxed planes. I was accountable for keeping the shed floor flawless and clean. Indeed, even the washroom latrines were essential for my obligations. So much for a long term higher education! I had some work and was grateful for itself and really delighted in working close to planes and individuals who cherished their work. I was paid $3 each hour and worked 8 hours out of every day or a sum of $24 hours of the, prior day charges.

The worker rate to fly the fundamental mentor, Piper Tomahawk, was $25 each hour. Work 8 hours, then, at that point, go fly 60 minutes. A make back the initial investment net increase cash shrewd however I was beginning to get the "flying bug". Basically I got a rebate on the flight educator. Leo didn't charge me!

What I recall most with regards to Leo, other than the "remove your arm at the shoulder" handshake, was his tender loving care when it came to flying. He was "old school" and requested that I regarded each part of flying and never underestimated wellbeing. I think it was whenever I first heard the articulation "close to 100% fatigue followed by 1% fear". He showed me never to let "carelessness creep in" when flying or "it could tear into you in the ass!" Something else I recollected and use for some things in my day to day existence was to "Be ready and consistently have a reinforcement plan". This is an ability I attempted to give to

my children today. Try not to anticipate that things should consistently turn out well for you and when they don't ensure you have a back-up arrangement.

Somewhere over Alaska during an excursion from JFK to NRT (Tokyo). Scott Weaver with AA. Boeing 777.

2014

eo was the primary educator to say to me. "Think ahead about the airplane or you're not kidding". This was the sort of thing I truly recognized as an understudy going through the high speed of pilot preparing flying the T-37 and actually the
supersonic T-38.

I don't how frequently Leo would say. "Follow the agenda, in any event, when you have a large portion of it retained". Today, as I fly the 777-200 to the profound South America, I actually recollect those illustrations.

I actually even apply a portion of those propensities to my day by day schedules, when I awaken and make my own "to do" really take a look at records.

All our flights were directed in a tiny and tight fitting next to each other coach. You really have more space in a VW slug-bug. Temperatures in the late spring in Redding, California were above and beyond 100 degrees with slope temperatures near 120 degrees. Like all starting pilots there was essential ground preparing to incorporate plane frameworks, power plant activities, flight instruments, optimal design standards, four powers of flight. The flying included security of flight, airspace, correspondence, radio methods, traffic design activities, map/diagram abilities, essential climate hypothesis, getting winds, climate perils, pressure height, weight and equilibrium, plane execution, route and dead retribution. We discussed human variables, physiology, navigation, flying crosscountry and significantly more. Generally, our flight interview would persist to the supper table. Then, at that point, off to bed, up at 0600 the following morning and back to the air terminal.

ooking back on my underlying flight preparing, my granddad showed me substantially more than the fundamentals of flying. He showed me crushing. The most effective method to get up regular and go to work, how to define objectives, record your objectives and afterward do whatever it took to accomplish your objectives. In one summer, I learned more than in four years at a college. From a man with an eighth grade training, Leo helped me to be enthusiastic with regards to something you love. He instructed me that flying is a combination of basic discipline and outright opportunity.

**

t's 1987 and only 45 years prior the United States was maneuvered into World War II to help our partners. What's more, only a couple of miles east of where we are today, emerged from the desert, the first of four flight preparing bases called Thunderbird Field where my granddad was a flight educator in the PT-17.

It's been north of a long time since I last saw Grandpa Leo, when he went to my Undergraduate Pilot (UPT) function at Vance AFB, Enid Oklahoma. After pilot preparing, I was chosen to get back to Vance as a T38 Instructor Pilot, frequently alluded to a First Assignment Instructor Pilot or FAIP. Presently Leo is remaining with us in Litchfield Park, Arizona, only south of the primary door at Luke AFB and simply a short drive to Thunderbird Field.

Earlier that day, Leo and I plunked down for espresso and breakfast.

When Leo inquires, "Enlighten me regarding your F16 preparing here at Luke and your graduation mission?"

"The preparation has been incredible and the stream far better." I start.

"The F16 B course is intended for pilots with no F16 experience, normally straight out of pilot preparing or such as myself, finishing a visit as an educator pilot. You realize it took me four years to complete pilot preparing, grandpa. One as an understudy and three as an educator." I laugh.

Leo giggles realizing that I'm making fun of myself.

"We're flying the third era of the F16C model, which is the single seat, and the D model which has two seats", I say.

"All fly by wire innovation" Leo says.

"Precisely!" I shout, presently realizing he has done his own examination.

"So becoming accustomed to the involved choke and side stick controls was a little unique feel, however practically normal, after your first flight. The genuine test is becoming accustomed to the flight, working the radar and different sensors on board as you're figuring out how to fly the stream," I proceed.

"Generally great stuff contrasted with that Piper Tomahawk we flew only a couple of years prior!" Leo adds as he takes a taste of his espresso.

We go through the principal month in test system with non military personnel project workers during the ground preparing stage," I proceed. "Very little not quite the same as what you did as a teacher over at Glendale. What was that like, ten miles from this very spot?" I notice.

Leo chuckles "That's right, north of 45 years prior? What's more, somewhat more mind boggling than the Stearman we were preparing our cadets in," he adds.

I laugh. "In any case, I bet everything were fundamentally something similar. We cover everything from agenda methodology, airplane instruments or flying crisis strategies presumably as you did in the connection mentors back in what… 1941?"

What was your preparation like in those days?" I inquire.

"All things considered, we took cadets essentially off the road with no flight insight. They were all volunteers, passed a flight physical and they were in an our preparation program. We were the main layer in the preparation pipeline, so after an intense ground school, assuming they passed, we'd give every cadet five or six preparing flights and in case they couldn't hack it, they were gone," Leo says with a smile.

"Gone? As in cleaned out?" I inquire.

"That's right, we didn't burn through much time. I'd say we lost around 30% of the folks who strolled through the front entryway. Assuming the cadet didn't make it the PT-17 program, he wasn't sent home. Good gracious, he was headed toward guide or bombardier preparing. There was a conflict continuing and it was everyone ready and available in those days, everybody was gotten a new line of work to help the work," he said.

"Those waste of time numbers were near the normal waste of time rate we have in our pilot preparing today," I add.

"Tomorrow we're arranging a genuinely mind boggling mission Grandpa," I start. "It's our graduation exercise and we get to drop "live" or genuine bombs. I can hardly wait."

start to clarify somewhat about the F16 RTU prospectus. First we get a couple of rides in the stream to settle in and afterward we take a contact/instrument check ride to ensure we're protected to take off and land. Then, at that point, we advance into the aerial period of the preparation program. "It's the 'building a house' idea. Construct the establishment first, then, at that point, get increasingly more perplexing as you continue in the preparation." I get a tad out of hand depicting everything about our preparation, however grandpa is by all accounts appreciating paying attention to me talking F16 in abundance… he's clearly pleased with me being a pilot and continuing in the family strides, yet in particular, he's glad I've tracked down my enthusiasm.

I keep on clarifying how the initial not many months of the program incorporate around 25 flights or forays, including fundamental warrior moves or BFM. As understudies, we fly against a solitary enemy, ordinarily another F16C or D model from a hostile, guarded or high-perspective or essentially head on battle. Every one of the flights are testing and you figure out how to regard the Viper's capacity to pull 9 g's.

Leo says, "9 g's? What's that like? I think the most we pulled in the Stearman was 4 to 5g's to do a circle. Obviously back then, we had no checks to let us know the number of g's we pulled and you could really pull the wings off the plane!"

I chuckle a little at my grandpa joke, and afterward continue with my clarification. "The aerial stage situations gets more perplexing in the accompanying ten trips as we called them, as we begin to cover strategic catch missions. During these flights, understudies fly in a two-transport development and convey versus a one, two and at times up to four enemies or "miscreants" who are mimicking Soviet strategies. There was one night catch mission with an aerial refueling mission.Talk about complex, yet testing missions."

"How can that air refuel in the fly?" Leo inquires.

"It's difficult. Getting your stream that near another enormous big hauler like the KC-135 and fundamentally freezing in that situation for three to five nerve wracking minutes, is testing". I don't think I took a breath the whole time. "Yet, we as a whole got past it and made due to move onto the following period of preparing."

The aerial piece of the schedule, gets done with commitment against divergent warriors. Up to this time, we've been battling against other F16C jets. "This was one of my features and most loved stories.

The Viper is fundamentally an enchanted fly." I tell Leo with a major grin in my face, the Viper after everything is my top pick.

"As you probably are aware, flying is a lot of three dimensional in reasoning. In any case, with the Viper, you contemplate being in a spot in space, and with full max engine propulsion and 6+ g's, you can place your stream in that piece of the sky." And obviously I'm utilizing two hands to depict to him the development in space. "The Viper causes pilots to feel extremely certain to put the stream precisely where they need to put the fly. It's that great in its plan, has that much power and ability that it's an enchanted stream and improves normal pilots," as I take a taste of espresso.

Let me give you an example."Last month, I'm planned to fly a 1 V 1, divergent mission against the Marines based out of Yuma, Az. They're flying the Israeli constructed Kfir or F21. It's a French plan , delta wing, more established age, all climate warrior. What's more, pilots flying are very much experienced, with throughout 10 years of contender time A4's, F14's and F18's. I don't know what's in store before the mission so I head to the "vault" or got weapons library, and study the subtleties of my foe . Their weapons ability. Turn sweep. Aerial rockets, and so on I don't track down much with regards to the fly, however I do get familiar with it's a delta wing, somewhat short reach and initially planned by Dassault Aviation with restricted turn ability. Tomorrow it will reproduce something in the Soviet stock from the 1970's with basic weapons and hotness detecting aerial rockets. A standard mission situation at this degree of preparing. Now, I'm simply eager to see another fly, other than the Viper. Preparing against another 9 g able stream is intense and hard on my kid neck" I snicker.

take a gander at Leo and his eyes are going to coat over, so I get him a top off on his espresso.

"Our first commitment was a 1 V 1, expressing 30 miles separated. A couple of scopes of the radar, I get him and start my offset of 30 degrees" As I utilize my hands to show my granddad the flight ways of the two planes. "We meet no holds barred, with my power out of gear, I make sure to jump out a couple of flares to overcome his hotness looking for rocket. I promptly start a hard turn and a slight move as I pull my lift vector towards the covering of his stream". My hands are getting mutilated now and wound. Leo comprehends my words, however he improves understanding by seeing my "hands" as I point towards the watch on my other hand.

"The Kfir is all the way out of energy, because of delta wing and absence of push. Inside less a moment of our no holds barred commitment, I'm ready to "saddle" up and put the flute player or weapon sight on the overhang of my adversary.

'Firearms… .track… .kill' I say on the UHF normal recurrence. Yet, incredibly right now, the Kfir pitches up and turns over and begins to go crazy towards the desert floor. As my eyes are currently totally open reasoning he might need to rescue. 'Knock it off, knock it off, knock it off' is a wellbeing call we make on the UHF normal recurrence to stop any preparation and guarantee nobody is getting killed today.

The Marine in the other stream, serenely empties his fly, kicks in some rudder, rolls wings switch and recaptures his velocity and flies out of his twist and says. 'No concerns, it typical in this fly! Give me a couple of moments and we are all set once more!'"

I let my granddad know how flabbergasted I was that the stream performed so well and I had film to demonstrate it. In any case, to the Marines and the Kfirs, guard, they were the "preparation help" for our central goal.

Leo rapidly reminds me. "Recall what I educated you regarding never being careless in ANY plane or it will tear into you in the ass!"

We both giggle hard as I recall him letting me know this in my first example and I submit his words to memory now. Exemplary Leo, he gets up, wishes me best of luck and shakes my hand, immovably and takes off to shower as I head out the entryway for my last preparing trip at Luke AFB.

At the finish of the course, for our graduation work out, we were relied upon to apply all that we found out with regards to weapons, strategies and convey live weapons on a reenacted focus in the Barry Goldwater range in Southern Arizona. F16C Graduation is a major occasion in the existence of a pilot. Family and visitors are completely welcomed to join in. They generally get a visit through the base and find out with regards to where their expense cash is going. Leo even gets a couple of moments in the test system where he is a "whiz".

F16C graduation with Scott and Leo. Luke AFB, AB. 1987

That evening after our graduation service, I pause for a minute to consider that I am so lucky to have had guides like Leo and my father. I tracked down my enthusiasm and had the option to finish them their fantastic avionics strides. From supporting missions in World War II, to Vietnam, to aiding put a man on the moon during the Apollo project, the two of them buckled down. Each mission had the help of thousands. In particular, they had the help of their families; without their penances this would be completely impossible.

Today I'm flying one of the world's best warriors With my family backing and many years of avionics information and large number of flight hours passed down to me, I have turned into an inheritance pilot of Thunderbird Field. The examples learned at Luke AFB were supported by the illustrations educated to me as an understudy pilot. They're the very illustrations that were educated to my father, Steve Rickert, and every one of the cadets who prepared at Thunderbird Field by Leo himself and by many other bold non military personnel educator pilots more than 40 years prior. The light is passed on, and the fire is radiating brilliantly and will keep on doing as such for quite a long time in the future.

313th Hahn AB, Germany. Fortunate Puppy Friday T-shirt day! (Skipper Scott Weaver, extreme left)

Photographs of Thunderbird Field

Len with Cadet "Spitfire" Clay 1943

Class 43-I Graduation Dance Card

Leo with paint and model of a PT-17

Leo sitting in 1927 Model T Speedster

Leo's summer primary class at Thunderbird I

Lee's 4th primary training class at Thunderbird I

*Leo with his cadets dressed in
their Class "A" uniforms*

To a swell guy. Vern

Cadet Willie's Hero Shot

*Southwest Airways Wings
for the China Dragon*

The Thunderbirds
By Terry Wofford

Two Chinese Cadets visit the Purintons

Falcon Field Instructors and staff

Jimmy Purinton Flying Service, 1929

Jimmy Purinton / Weaver Wings and medals

Cadet with girlfriend

Falcon Field Flight Line

PT-17 Airborne

PT-17 #18 Falcon Field

Chinese Cadet visit Leo and Dot.

F16C #383, Captain Scott Weaver's.
Hahn AB, Germany

American Airlines Flagship Poster

DCANG Northern Watch deployment.
Kuwait, 1996

Thunderbird Cadets play baseball.

Southwest Airways
Official Welcome Handbook

AMRAAM Missile launch.
Major Scott Weaver, 1997.

*Leo Purinton (sweater) flight training with
DeVery, 1927.*

*Richard "Doc" Weaver. Basic Flight training
with Leo Purinton.*

Lt. Col RC Weaver. Veterans Day Speech.
North Carolina. 2016.

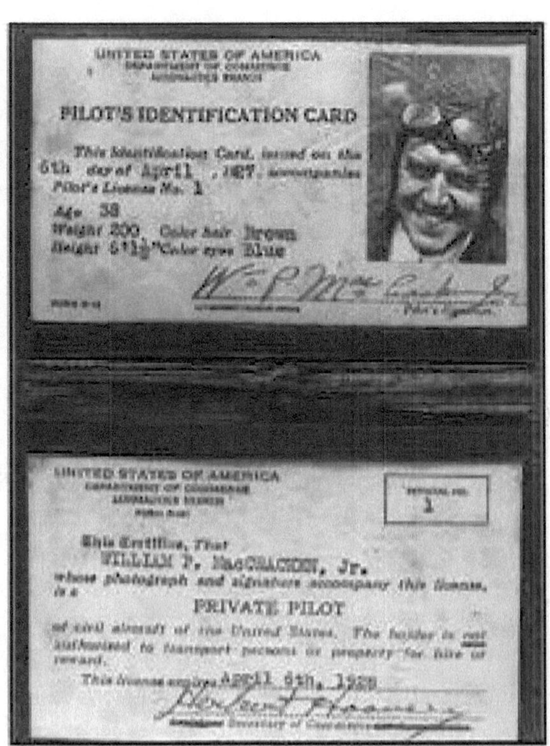

CAA Pilot ID #1.
William P. MacCracken, Jr.

2nd Lt. Scott Weaver, Vance AFB, OK

Captain RC Weaver and
C123 Crew Chief (unknown)

Thunderbird Cadet Floyd Hoenoelaar

*Cadets weekend off with
Leo and Dot Purinton*

Leo Purinton (arms crossed) with Cadets

*Jimmy Puritan (cockpit) Commercial Flight.
Medford, OR.*

April 1942. Vol 1- No. 2.
The Thunderbird newsletter.

March 1942. Vol 1- No. 1.
The Thunderbird newsletter.